A Rose among Thorns

A Daughter of Haiti

A Novel by

Ed Schwartz

First Edition - 2018

Bluffton, Indiana

First Editor Copyright – 2018
by Ed Schwartz

ISBN: 978-0-9907862-8-3

Copyrighted Material

Dedication

A Rose among Thorns

is dedicated to the 300,000

restavek children of Haiti

who have taught me much about

adversity, abuse, exploitation,

survival, broken-hearts,

compassion, love and family.

Introduction

*A **restavek** (or **restavec**) is a child in Haiti who is sent by his or her parents to work for a host household as a domestic servant because the parents lack the resources required to support the child. The term comes from the French language rester avec, "to stay with". Parents unable to care for children may send them to live with wealthier (or less poor) families; often their own relatives or friends. Often the children are from rural areas and relatives who host restaveks live in more urban ones. The expectation is that the children will receive food and housing (and sometimes an education) in exchange for doing housework. However, many restaveks live in poverty, may not receive proper education, and are at grave risk for physical, emotional, and sexual abuse. The restavek system is tolerated in Haitian culture, but not considered to be preferable. The practice meets formal international definitions of modern day slavery and child trafficking, and affects an estimated 300,000 Haitian children. The number of CDW (Child Domestic Workers) in Haiti, defined as: 1) living away from parents' home; 2) not following normal progression in education; 3) working more than other children, is more than 400,000.*

Wikipedia https://en.wikipedia.org/wiki/restavek

Though Haiti is an incredibly beautiful country and the people are some of the most generous, faithful and loving people I know, there is a dark side under the surface which exists in every country on earth.

Having the opportunity over many years to hear hundreds of heart-breaking stories from restaveks sparked the passion to share a composite of their lives. Though *A Rose among Thorns* is a work of fiction, the details are unfortunately all too factual.

A Rose among Thorns is shared through the parallel and intertwined lives of five restavek children, Rose, Jesulah, Jean Pierre, Joseph and Evens. They are truly the *'Sons and Daughters of Haiti'* waiting for freedom, hope, opportunity and a loving family.

Hopefully, awareness about restavek issues will create Haitian and international impetus to move away from a cultural practice bred by poverty and a reluctance to change the status quo. - *Ed Schwartz*

Chapter 1

Rose

Her short and shallow breaths came in raspy waves of gut-wrenching agony as she strained to find a relaxed position which would reduce the pain. The tossing, turning and never-ending search for relief didn't seem to help. The pain only seemed to get worse. She tried to remain still.

In the stifling heat and quiet darkness she tried desperately to make sense of where she was. Her small hands clutched at the rough burlap sack beneath her thin and fragile body. Reaching beyond the coarse cloth, her grasping fingers grabbed a handful of Haitian soil.

Then, a soothing hand gently touched her feverish and damp forehead and she heard the old woman's voice, "Rose, Rose... try to relax. You've been hurt and I'm trying to help you."

A mournful whimper escaped like a fading whisper from Rose's lips. Rose recognized the voice of Joanna. Tears filled the old woman's eyes as she splashed cool water on Rose's face and neck. She thought, "No twelve-year-old girl should have to go through this."

Rose's forehead was hot. The horrendous beating Rose had endured had broken a few ribs. The shallow breathing over the last two days had taken its toll and Rose had pneumonia.

When Joanna had undressed Rose to tend to the knife stabbing to her stomach, she saw the knotted scars on her back and arms. It brought back unwanted, pushed-back memories of her own difficult experiences as a young restavek slave girl two generations ago. Those nightmarish memories and what she was seeing in this brave girl brought her to tears. She wept silently as she tended to Rose.

The old woman's kindness and the cool water were having a calming effect. Rose slowly began to relax.

Joanna sadly knew there was no money to pay for a motorcycle taxi to get her to the distant clinic. Even if she would have had the money to pay for the taxi, she doubted Rose would survive the grueling trip. She resigned herself to do what she could to make her as comfortable as possible.

Rose looked upward through openings in the ill-maintained thatch roof at the stars. The faraway tiny spots of light ebbed and flowed, reminding her of the warm Caribbean waves which continually crept up to the southwest Haiti shoreline.

In the quietness between her rasping breaths, she tried to imagine the waves breaking at the beach. She wished she could be lying there instead of here in Joanna's hut. But, the beaches were many miles away and maybe a lifetime ago, or so it seemed. She was thankful to have someone caring for her.

Joanna knew Rose was on a precarious ledge, hovering between this life and the one to come. She was in God's hands and Joanna would do what she could to help.

As the cool water and the tender touch of Joanna's hands comforted her, the throbbing pain began to lessen.

Then, slowly, Rose felt herself being sluggishly yet persistently drawn to memories of another time, another place, and other people. She felt her mind slip-sliding away into darkness. The past began to fill her mind and memories started to arrive like fluttering butterflies...

Chapter 2

Rose - Six years earlier

      The warm tropical sun beat down on Rose's small six-year-old back. She loved how it seemed to warm her from the inside out. In a peculiar way it brought a kind of strange comfort to her. Other people seemed always to pursue shady and cool refuge from the incessant sticky heat, but she thrived in the hot Haitian sun. The rays and heat of the sun seemed to wrap itself around her.

      The sun was much like her family. Both were warm, comforting and full of life. She loved her family for the security, love and hope it brought.

      Sitting in the hot sun reminded her of a recent and special, unforgettable time with her sweet mama. Her mama was always incredibly busy. Taking care of five little girls was no small task and Mama was again pregnant. She was always busy with the ever-present chores of washing their meager clothing, finding food and making meals.

      One of the main time-takers for most Haitian families was the hard work of bringing water from the river. However, Mama never had to get the water for their drinking, washing and bathing. That was Rose's daily job.

      But, on one particular sunny and hot day, Mama chose to walk with Rose to the river a half-mile away to get fresh water. They talked about many things, some important and some not, and Rose's heart happily soaked in the priceless time. It wasn't often any of the girls got private time with their mama.

      When they arrived at the river, they looked for the men who were washing their trucks, motorcycles or tap-tap taxi's.

They looked for the young boys who were washing their cows. They scanned the riverbanks for anyone butchering an animal next to the river. Here and there were a few pigs wallowing in the rivers mud banks. Then, they carefully moved farther upstream to where the cleanest water awaited them.

They removed their clothing and jumped into the river. It was the first time Rose and her mama had actually had fun together. They noisily splashed each other and Rose gently washed her mama's back. When Mama washed her back, Rose felt a closeness and love she had never felt before. Rose was feeling very privileged to have this quality time with her busy mama. Rose laughed at her mama's large pregnant stomach. They talked about whether it was a boy or a girl.

Mama said, "I'm not sure what I'd do with a boy. After having five girls, it would be easier to just have another girl. But, who knows? I know your papa would be ready for a son."

They dried off in the hot sun, got dressed and filled two buckets with water.

Mama sat down on the riverbank. Rose joined her. Mama's face was full of sadness as she watched the many children wearily getting water. She pointed at them and said, "Most of those children are restaveks."

"What's a restavek?"

"Oh, restavek is the name we give to the really poor children who no longer can live with their family but who stay with someone else."

"Why do children have to leave their family to live somewhere else?"

"Often, the family can no longer care for their own children. Their mamas and papas love the children so much they give them away, so the children can have a better life."

"I can understand it'd be sad, but right now you seem really, really sad."

"Ah, my Rose. You may be a six-year-old child, but you see things other people don't see. There's an old Haitian saying, *'To hear and to see are two different things.'*"

"Mama, what does that mean?"

"Many people hear things, but fail to understand them in their heart. Many people see things, but don't learn from them. I think you're able to hear, see and learn. But, I think you're also able to understand these things in your heart. I want you to remember these restavek children and understand how difficult their lives are."

"Did you ever know any restavek children?"

Mama waited a minute. Was Rose ready to hear this? "Yes, I was a restavek when I was young."

"What was it like?"

Again, there was a moment's hesitation. "It was a horrible time for me. I loved my family very much and leaving them was the most terrible day in my life. The years as a restavek were hard. Things happened I can't talk about. They're better left in the past and not spoken of."

Rose's eyes filled with tears as she saw the hurt in her mama's face and sensed the sadness in her heart. "Will I become a restavek?"

"No, no, no! Life is difficult for us as a family, but we're getting by. Tough times will come, but you'll have your mama and papa to take care of you."

Rose turned her eyes to the river and watched the children she now knew as restavek. She thought she could identify them from the other children. She could see the difference in their faces. They were full of sadness and their bodies were small and thin. The restavek children weren't playing in the water or talking to others. They were simply and hurriedly taking care of their work. As she looked in their eyes, they seemed empty. In fact most didn't make eye contact with her or anyone else.

As Mama turned and watched Rose's face, she saw the hurt and compassion grow in her oldest daughter's eyes. She wondered if she'd gone too far in sharing her own past hurts and sufferings with her six-year-old.

She said, "Rose, I think you'll someday be one who will care deeply about the last, lost, least and lonely."

Mama took a shirt, soaked it in the river and spun it into a long spiral cloth. She carefully coiled it on Rose's hair and lifted a bucket to the top of her head. Soon, the never-ending daily task of carrying water from the river would give her strong neck muscles. Years of walking the rough stone paths barefoot would give her strong and calloused feet. The weight of the bucket squeezed water from the cloth and cooled Rose's head as it dribbled down her face. Mama took another shirt, soaked and coiled it on her own head.

They began the half-mile walk back to their hut with the two buckets of water. Rose's heart was bursting with love for her mama. She could look in her mama's eyes and sense the deep love from her. The only bad thing about this trip to the river was the tragedy she saw in the lives of the child-slaves, the restavek children. Her young and soft heart broke for them.

Chapter 3

Her family's hut was only 200' from the Caribbean so Rose spent much of her time dawdling on the beach. The clear blue water was always a warm and fascinating draw for her.

Since the ground was sandy near the beach, men couldn't grow crops. Just a mile inland however, rice thrived in paddies, but along the shoreline nothing of substance would grow well. Generally, their family livelihood was the sea. Excessive fishing and pollution took its toll on the sea life, so being a fisherman was a hard and sparse life. Here and there, wooden dugout boats were sitting on the white sand waiting for their next outing. Nets were lying on the sand waiting for repair or ready for the next excursion. Lobsters, octopus, fish and briny shrimp would be the sustenance of the day for the fishermen and their families.

Sitting on the hot white sand, she looked over her shoulder at her family's small hut. It was one room, had palm-thatched walls, a rusty, dilapidated, corrugated tin roof, a dirt floor, one bed and an outdoor cooking area. The hut leaked like a sieve during rain storms and the thatch had to be replaced often, but it was home. Even though the floor was dirt, it was packed like concrete. Mama diligently swept it every day.

Rose's papa had begun squatting on this small piece of land, owned by the government, years ago. No one had ever objected. The sandy soil wasn't able to grow crops. Though the view was beautiful and living on the beach was great for Rose, it was simply a place for the poorest of the poor. No one, at least no one in their right mind, would live where the hurricanes could reach them and place themselves purposely in harm's way.

The terror and memory of last year's hurricane still haunted her. The unseen wind had begun blowing harder and stronger. The normally gentle lapping waves near their hut would soon be crashing like thunder. The incessant rain, which began with small sprinkles would increase to a blinding torrent. It would become like a vertical river flowing from the dark swirling sky.

As the huge storm approached, Rose, then five-years-old, was worried about her younger sisters. As the oldest of the five girls, Rose automatically took on the task of being the chief worrier and master protector. Papa and Mama had predictably produced a child each year. Rose picked up the vulnerable baby and held her close.

Papa packed a few meager things in a backpack and walked his family two miles inland to escape the anticipated and coming fury of yet another hurricane.

Rose remembered the lesson her papa had taught her that day about the hurricane. She had asked, "Papa, why do we have to leave our home? We can stay inside and be safe."

"Ah, my Rose. There's an old Haitian proverb which says, *'When the wind blows you can see the hens behind.'*"

"I don't understand. What does that mean?"

"It means even the chickens are wise enough to get their heads out of the coming storm and move away from it. All you'll see of smart chickens are their rear ends."

Then Papa continued, "Rose, you've always been one to question things. I think you'll be a wise woman someday. I'm glad you're asking questions."

When they returned a day after the hurricane's wrath, Rose was shocked to see so many trees down. Those remaining had lost their leaves and coconuts. Even the huge, strong mango trees were shredded. Sadly she knew losing those mangoes and coconuts would make their food supply dwindle. Was there no end to tragedy and poverty in Haiti?

Then she saw their hut, or rather, where their hut had been. No roof. No sides. Their possessions, including their one and only bed were gone. The hurricane had no mercy.

The clean-up began. They searched and searched for cooking utensils, tools, clothing and anything else of value. In the rubble of nearby downed trees and palm leaves they found a pot, pan and small shovel, but they didn't belong to Papa. With a smile, he picked them up anyway.

Rose said, "Papa, those things don't belong to us. We can't take them."

"Rose, there's an ancient Haitian proverb which says, 'To get by isn't a sin.'"

Again Rose said, "I don't know what that means."

"*Degaje* is a word you need to learn. It means '*to make do.*' Since we're so poor, it's important to survive by almost any means possible. This pot, pan and shovel I found are now ours. Someone else is picking up our tools somewhere else. Others are now the owners of our things. Learn degaje well, because life will be difficult and you'll have to make do. Not only will you have to make do for yourself, you'll need to let others make do for themselves."

He continued, "Rose, I respect how you're trying to do what's right. I think someday you'll be a woman of integrity. So, maybe you won't only be a wise woman, but also a just woman."

It seemed to Rose her mama and papa were expecting great things of her. She felt honored to know they trusted and respected her. She loved her family.

It had been an incredibly hard day. Rose realized her family would need to start over and that would mean building another home as quickly as possible. If they didn't establish their home soon, someone else would start squatting on their small dirt pad.

The first thing Papa needed to do was find palm fronds suitable for building his walls and roof. The home's hard-earned tin was likely now inland a mile or so and already claimed by a happy family. Papa wasn't overly upset by the loss of his roof because he had found his tin after an earlier hurricane. It seemed the rusty, bent and dilapidated tin roof just went from one owner to another as often as another hurricane struck. It wasn't difficult for him to remember the joy he had felt when finding that tin two years earlier.

While scrounging and searching for useful items, Rose's four-year-old sister Marie squealed. "Rose, Rose, I found your doll!"

Rose eagerly ran over to Marie who was excitedly pointing at a small girl who was holding the doll Papa had made for her when she was three. She walked over to the neighboring girl and reached for the doll. The girl pulled the doll close to her chest and clutched it tightly.

Rose looked over expectantly to Papa who was watching. She looked again at the little girl holding her doll.

Rose forced a smile, patted the girl on the head and walked away. She knew the little girl was 'making do.'

Papa said, "Rose, there's an old proverb which says, *'Even when you give a little, you're not being cheap.'* You're learning so much at a young age. I think you'll be a wise, just and compassionate woman someday."

Rose said, "Isn't there an end to the proverbs you and Mama know?"

"No, we live by proverbs. The wisdom of our fathers and grand-fathers was passed down from those before them when our ancestors were slaves for the French and Spanish. Those early African slaves couldn't read or write, so they memorized one another's wisdom and shared it with their children, over and over again. Just like I'm doing with you. You'll share those things with your children someday."

Her heart felt warm and safe as she talked with her papa. He loved her very much and she loved him even more.

Chapter 4

It was mid-morning and the sun was already warming the muddy and green rice paddies. Looking north across the flat lowlands toward the mountains, the rice was in various stages of growth. Some paddies were muddy mounds, ready to receive the wisps of stalky rice. Others were already harvested with the empty straws strewn off to the side. Some were soon ready for harvest. Rose never tired of watching the men stomping the mud, preparing the ground for one of the much needed staples of Haiti, rice.

The sun was also warming the many stately mango trees. Some were huge and had been producing fruit for many, many years. Papa had told Rose that some of the trees producing fruit in southwest Haiti began when the slaves were still working the sugar cane plantations. He had said some have produced their sweet fruit for almost 300 years.

Rose sat on the lumpy ground with her back to her mama under one of those stately and shady trees. Mama was sitting on a short, palm tree stump and was ready to braid Rose's hair. Mama's skirt was gracefully tucked between her legs with Rose neatly fitting between her knees.

Hair braiding time was a perfect opportunity to share the rich and living history of family, proverbs and Haiti. Sometimes it seemed this time wasn't about braiding hair at all. It was a bonding time with mothers and daughters.

As Mama started with the first braid, she said, "You look like me when I was six-years-old. For this first braid, I'll talk of my life as a child. When I was your age, my papa told me I was beautiful. He told me someday I'd have children who looked like me. He was right. We were very poor and I had to work every day in the rice paddies. My father didn't own the land or the rice, but was paid by another man to work his paddy."

Finished with the first braid, Mama moved to the second. "My mother who was your grandmother, told me her life had been very difficult. Her papa died when she was a baby, so she never knew him. Her mother tried very hard to keep her family together. With seven children she had many tough times, but her brothers helped to keep her family together. My mama died before you were born."

The third braid began. "Talking about family reminds me to tell you about lakou. Lakou has a very deep meaning. It can mean 'yard' or 'neighborhood.' As you look up from where you are, you see a few homes close by. They are in our 'yard', but at the same time, we are in their 'yard.'

The other meaning of the word lakou is about taking care of one another. Haitians care for each other. I watch my neighbor's children and they watch mine. It's like all the children belong to all of us. If anyone in the lakou has a problem, we all carry the problem together. There's an old proverb which says, *'A lot of small potatoes make a heavy load, but many hands make the load light.'*

The braiding continued. A fourth gave the opportunity to talk about her mama's personal struggles; another about Rose; another about her restavek years; yet another about Rose's future children; and the braids continued.

Rose loved the braiding time. She had heard some of the old and rich stories before. She could visualize herself sitting under this mango tree braiding her daughter's hair and sharing these same stories with her. The history of Haiti would continue from generation to generation.

These special times with her mama were precious. Rose felt nothing else in the world mattered as long as she had her papa, mama and family.

~

Sitting in the soft and damp sand, Rose began burying her wriggly toes and then her legs. Lying back, she sprawled in the sand and soaked up the sun. She was glad last year's hurricane was over and they had made a new beginning. There was no tin roof, but the new thatch kept them somewhat dry.

A small crab made its way slowly along the beach and came close. Rose remained as quiet as she could as it crawled over one sand-covered leg and plummeted to the sand valley between her knees. Though crabs were a part of the local food chain, she couldn't bear to interrupt this crab's happy meanderings.

She felt almost a camaraderie with the lonely and focused crab. Both of them were small, vulnerable and hungry.

It was then she heard her mother's scream from the hut. Quickly emerging from the sand coffin she had buried herself in, she stood up. She was careful to not hurt her new crab-friend in spite of the urgency of the scream.

The scream was her mama's natural reaction to the pain of bringing another child into the world. Rose remembered the last two births but not those before.

She ran to the hut with a giddy smile and growing excitement to welcome a new sister or brother into their growing family.

She saw her papa fidgeting anxiously outside the front door beside two older women who were her aunts. The screams from the hut dwindled.

A few minutes later, a woman who Rose recognized from a neighboring village soon emerged from the hut holding a baby wrapped in a towel. She held the wriggling new baby up to Papa's waiting arms.

Almost in slow motion, Rose saw her papa's large and rough hands tremble as he accepted his new and additional responsibility in the form of this new baby. He opened the towel to see he finally had his long awaited son.

Moise looked at his son with pride, a grin, and gratitude knowing his family name would continue into the future. With a bit of a selfish thought, he also knew having a strong son in the family would give him security in his old age. Though daughters would add value to a family, a son brought future hope and revenue. Rose saw joy in her papa's eyes.

Then, he raised those proud, happy eyes and looked into the face of the midwife. Rose saw his eyes transition from joy to concern and then to horror. Moise knew immediately something was horrendously wrong. Barging his way past the midwife, he rushed into his hut.

His wife, the mother of his now six children was lying on their simple bed. He looked from her face to the ground, where there were towels and sheets covered with blood. Seeing his wife's ashen face and her closed eyes, he knew life would never be the same for him and his family. His wife was gone.

He placed his newborn son carefully into the outstretched hands of the midwife and slowly knelt beside his wife. His sobs came immediately as he touched her face. Moise wept for the loss of his wife. He wept for his six children. He wept as his expectations of having a long life with his wife were now crushed and rapidly disappearing. He wept at the thought of raising six children without a wife. He wept for his poverty and inability to take her to a clinic to bear their children. He wept for what he knew was to come.

Rose was confused. She had been through this before. The life-giving screams from the hut at childbirth weren't new. The presentation of a wrinkly, crying baby to her papa had happened before. Her papa going into the hut to be with her mama was expected.

But what was the wailing coming from the hut? What possibly could have gone wrong? What had happened to my papa? Has something happened to my mama?

Rose's aunt pulled her aside, sat on the ground and held her tightly. Why is my aunt crying? Looking up she saw other women from the village holding her four sisters. Why are all these people crying?

Then Rose saw her sisters crying. They had no idea what was happening, but crying seemed to be the reaction. Rose couldn't control her confused and muddled emotions. The tears came and spilled onto the dirt in front of her hut. The same hut which had been so full of safety, security, hope and family was now filled with the sobs of her papa.

Rose's tiny shoulders rose and fell, again and again. With her hands covering her face, she gave in to her emotions and silently wept.

Chapter 5

It seemed forever before her papa slowly emerged through the single door of their hut. Rose was shocked and thought he looked like an old man. His normally strong shoulders were stooped. His head hung. His chin nearly rested on his chest.

He raised his hand over his eyes to shield them from the glaring sun as he began to slowly look around. He saw Rose and his four other daughters crying. He fell helplessly to his knees in the dirt. Now, he felt a weight on his shoulders which was too heavy for a man to carry.

Rose was scared. She had never seen her papa like this. He was always strong, humorous and in control. She quickly rose from her aunt's ample lap and went to him. A desperate Moise grabbed his oldest daughter and held her tightly. Rose felt crushed as her Papa clutched her. It was like he couldn't bear to lose anything else in his life.

Moise's world had just been shattered. In typical Haitian or African culture the role of a wife and mother is enormous. The father would seek work at meager jobs in the area to bring home a few coins to his family. Those few Haitian coins called gourdes would purchase a small amount of rice, beans or food items he couldn't produce himself. With almost 75% of Haitian people having no meaningful employment, it was very difficult and competitive finding any work at all. The thought of his family potentially starving kept him away from home for most of the day.

While he had been away at those odd jobs, the home ran like clockwork under his wife's direction. She'd be busy finding food and preparing it, mending and washing clothing, keeping five little girls under control and safe, and keeping the hut clean and in shape. Her work never stopped even when she was about to give birth.

How would he be able to find work during the day and still take care of raising his growing family? Who would care for his newborn son? Who would nurse him? How would those five little girls survive?

Some families were able to send their children to kindergarten, but he could never raise enough money to make that happen. As he thought about the future, he wept again. Rose felt awkward patting her papa on the back, comforting him. Her heart broke watching him suffer.

Finally, he stood up. He called his other daughters to him. Rose picked up her youngest sister who was barely one-year-old. It was an incredibly sad scene. A man with his five daughters and a newborn son in the arms of a midwife, standing together, outside what was once a home filled with joy.

~

Moise felt hopeless. It had been a long and hard week since Mama had died. The week had been chaotic, sad and full of unknowns. He tried desperately to get into a routine which would permit his six children to feel safe again.

Moise had no idea international statistics placed Haiti as the highest maternal mortality rate for the entire western hemisphere. Pregnancy in Haiti is a dangerous thing.

Infant mortality is worse, with almost sixty babies out of one thousand dying at birth. Absence of qualified medical staff, sanitation and the lack of medicine contribute greatly to the numbers. In rural Haiti, death is an often and sad fact of life.

Moise knew of many babies over the years who had never gotten their first glimpse of the beauty of Haiti. He had witnessed the grief of many parents who had lost a child, or two or three. But now, he knew a deeper grief. The loss of his wife jeopardized the lives of his six children. He realized he was in a life and death struggle which wasn't going to end today or tomorrow.

He thought back a few days to when Mama was laid to rest in the green and white, above-ground, concrete tomb. The tombs were used over and over. The end would be broken out, the body inserted and cement and stucco would seal it again. Bodies over time decomposed and made room for new occupants.

The funeral procession down the country road had been long. It seemed many wanted to help carry the load of grief his family was carrying. Moise's brother carried his youngest daughter. Moise carried his newborn son. The other four girls held hands and walked beside their papa. The area hadn't seen a sadder sight for a long time. When his wife was sealed behind the fresh concrete stucco, he wept again. He wondered if he'd be so busy caring for his family he'd have no time or energy to grieve her loss.

On the way back to his hut, the procession had gradually dwindled as his neighbors and friends stopped at their own lakou and homes. Finally arriving at home, alone with his six children, he opened the door to a dark and empty room. Again, Moise wept.

Rose interrupted Moise's grief and his wandering thoughts. "What should I fix for our meal, Papa?"

The neighbors had been generous this past week. Every day someone had brought them rice and beans, plantains and a few mangoes. Their lakou neighbors were helping him carry the load.

Moise said, "The first thing we need is water. Take your sister Marie and bring back as much as you can."

Getting water from the river wasn't a new thing for Rose, but taking her younger sister was. They each took two small buckets and headed east to the river. It was a well-worn path which took them a half-mile past many lakous and huts.

The river was like life. Always changing. When it rained in the mountains, flash floods quickly and powerfully rushed down to the Caribbean. This 200' wide ravine would carry many rocks, boulders and tree trunks along with the rushing water. When it was a dry season, the river would have a few small places where water ran. Today it was nearly dry.

As Rose and Marie approached the river, they stopped on the steep bank. They looked across the wide expanse of rocks and gravel bars making up the river bottom, to the very large village on the other side. They could see many huts almost touching one another, beginning at the ravine edge, stretching east.

Rose said to Marie, "Papa told me that life in that large village is more difficult than it is for us. There are many, many poor people living there. I'm glad we live on the beach. Papa said that each year when the monsoon comes, homes along these cliffs crumble into the river. That would be a horrible thing to see happen to your home!"

Then they looked down. Rose showed Marie the path to the bottom. It was steep but they made it without falling. It seemed to Rose that everything was difficult in Haiti. Already she was dreading the climb up with their load of water.

When they got to the bottom, Rose said, "Mama told me an old proverb, *'Water doesn't cross over holes. First the holes must be filled before passing beyond.'*"

Marie said, "I don't understand."

"Do you see the many holes in the riverbed where men dug out rocks, sand and gravel for making concrete or for filling in the roads? Sometimes there will be water in the river and you can't see the holes. You must be careful to only walk where you can see the bottom. If you fall into one of those holes, you won't be able to climb out."

Sadly, Rose realized she was now in a role of teaching her sister the things her mother would have taught. For a moment, Rose felt proud to be able to share a proverb. But the pride was quickly pushed aside by a deep sadness as she thought about the riverside time she had with her mama not so long ago. Then, just as suddenly, the sadness was roughly shoved aside by an anger which surprised her.

The emotions this past week were as varied and complicated as the countryside of Haiti. Mountains, valleys, flat places, dry places, rocky areas, deserts and jungles.

Marie interrupted her thoughts and said, "Rose, I'm hungry."

"We'll be home soon and I'll fix us a meal."

Arriving home, they were surprised to see Papa kneeling in front of their canvas-covered outdoor cooking area. The rocks on the ground corralled a pile of hot charcoal that was now heating two pots.

Papa said, "I have a surprise. I decided to see if I could cook. In a little while, we'll have rice, beans and sauce."

Five-year-old Marie laughed, "Papa, since I'm hungry, I'll eat, but I don't think it will taste like Mama's food."

Rose was glad to see her sister giggle. She was even happier to hear her papa laugh aloud. It took the rough edges off her own anger, sadness and grief. She guessed it was doing the same for Papa and Marie.

She heard a noise from the hut. With a questioning look to Papa, he smiled and said, "Your mama's friend Fabiola is feeding your little brother. You can tell her hello."

Rose opened the door. Seeing Fabiola was like connecting to her own mama again. She had many great memories of Mama, Fabiola and their other friends talking and laughing in the lakou.

Fabiola and Mama had been pregnant at the same time and Fabiola had delivered a little girl two months earlier. When Mama died, she had offered to nurse Rose's little brother. Now, Fabiola was sitting in the chair nursing two babies. It was a life-giving and sacrificial act for her to offer and then to actually do. The amount of time required was huge, especially since she had her own baby to feed, as well as caring for her family.

Rose was only just beginning to understand the concept of lakou. It seemed like most people she knew were quick to help others in deep and meaningful ways.

Around the world, cultures fall into two broad categories being either *individualistic* or *collectivist*. Western cultures such as in the United States, fall in the individualistic category. Goals, purpose and passions tend to be personal and independent of others. In a collectivist society like Haiti and most developing nations, people are interdependent on one another. Everything is about relationships first and end-goals are nearly always in second place.

As Rose watched Fabiola nursing her un-named little brother, her heart warmed. Not everything in life was bad or difficult.

As Fabiola watched Rose, she asked, "What are you thinking about?"

Pausing a moment, Rose said, "I'm thinking about my mama. I remember her, my sisters remember her, but my brother will never know her."

"That's true. But your brother has his mother living inside of him. You'll see her in him as he gets older. She left part of herself in all of her children."

Fabiola continued, "Your mama talked of you often."

"Really? What did she say?"

"I think she may have told you already."

"I'm not sure I know the things you're talking about."

"Well, I'll remind you. She said you're the oldest child and you're a leader. She told me she watched your sadness one day at the river when you learned about restavek children. She thought you would be one to always love and care for the last, lost, least and lonely."

"I remember her saying that, not so long ago."

"She said you were a stubborn girl. Not stubborn like a donkey, but like someone who never gives up. She said you're more like a crab. Always moving around and always busy doing something."

Rose laughed and said, "I'm glad she said I'm not like a donkey!"

"Your mama said you'd be a wise woman wanting to do the right things. She said your heart was made of smiles and compassion."

Rose smiled broadly and realized maybe she did have her mama inside of her.

Chapter 6

The days and weeks rolled by. Somehow, someway, they survived as a family. Moise found work periodically. It seemed many knew of his struggles as a man with many children and no wife.

One day, as he waited in a group of men waiting to be picked for a small job, a young man was selected next to him. The young man hesitated and told Moise to take the work. He said, "As a single man, I'll get by." Moise was humbled and touched.

Those kinds of experiences gave Moise and his young family hope.

Rose's days were long when Papa was away trying to find work. Mama's duties had now became her duties. When Rose would get water, five-year-old Marie watched the rest of the children. Of course, all the children were under the watchful eyes of the neighboring lakou mothers and families.

When Rose returned from the river, there was the never ending mending and washing of clothes, getting food ready, cleaning the hut and of course, heading back to the river for more water.

The children were always excited when Papa returned home. He almost always had something for the family to eat when he arrived. Sometimes it was more, sometimes it was less. On the days it was 'less', he seemed quiet. On the days it was 'more', he knew how to make them laugh and they loved it.

One evening as darkness approached, it was only Rose sitting with her papa outside the hut talking. Rose said, "Papa, how did I get my name?"

Papa paused and then said, "Your mama and I were excited to know we had a baby coming. We talked about it often. We wondered if we would have a boy or a girl. We thought if you were a boy we would name you Rooster, Mule or Goat. But, God surprised us as we had a beautiful girl, so we had to find a different name."

Rose laughed along with her papa.

"You were so beautiful. When you were born, your skin was almost red, different than the beautiful brown you are today. After a few days, we decided to always remember you as our beautiful red-skinned baby girl, so we called you Rose."

Rose hadn't heard the story before. She raised an arm and looked at the skin and was thankful she was no longer red.

Papa continued, "As I've watched you grow, I'm glad we named you Rose. A rose is a beautiful flower. You started out as a little bud, but you've blossomed into something very beautiful. A rose bush has hundreds of thorns and only a few flowers. I've often thought as I see the difficult times of Haitian life that you're just like a rosebush. You're a beautiful flower surrounded by thorns. You're my Rose."

Rose got up from her seat in the dirt and crawled into her papa's lap. He held her close. Both were hoping this moment would forever be remembered and would never change. But, both separately, were feeling a shadow slowly enveloping their family. Both remembered the proverb, *'Live today but think about tomorrow.'*

Life seemed to continue on as usual, except for desperately missing a mother and wife. There were changes happening, but they were subtle.

Papa was growing quieter. Finding work became more difficult for him. It seemed people were beginning to forget he had lost his wife and was caring for six children. After all, it had been over two years already.

Rose was now eight-years-old and little Riderson was two. Rose was glad when Papa had named him Riderson instead of Goat, Rooster or Mule.

As Rose and Marie made their way to the river for water, they would continually see other children. The girls they saw were dressed in checkerboard dresses of blue and white, with blue and white ribbons in their hair. The boys had matching blue and white checked shirts. All were on their way to school with small backpacks filled with the pencils, notebooks and textbooks needed to bring them future success and hope.

Two-thirds of Haiti's children enter kindergarten. Only eight per-cent graduate from high school. With 75% of Haitians not having meaningful employment, even the educated children would have a difficult time finding a job. There remained little hope for Moise's uneducated children.

Moise was well aware, without education his children would continue to languish in the poverty he experienced, as had his father before him and his father before that. Some things didn't seem to change.

He was also aware that without his children having an education and little likelihood of employment, their ability to support him in his old age would be remote.

When Moise got home that day, Rose asked, "Papa, will there ever be a chance for me to go to school?"

It was a heart-breaking question for him to deal with. He said, "Most children start school at three or four-years-old. You're already five years beyond that. The cost of clothes and books for one child is more than I have. I already have four children who could be in school."

He paused and sadly said, "I don't see how I can ever send you children to school."

Rose said, "I understand. I know we're not the only ones not going to school."

"You're a very special girl, Rose. You understand so much and you never complain. I don't know what I'd do without you. You've learned so much about life. You're like a mama to the other children and I'm amazed how you're teaching Marie all the things you know."

Rose soaked up the praise like she used to soak up the sun at the beach. She was so busy now that her days of crab-watching or sun-basking were few and far between. Occasionally she still got away, but now the other children followed her there. But, it was okay, as they were such a part of who she was.

She thought about her sisters and brother. Marie at seven-years-old was rapidly learning how to care for the other children as well as caring for the home.

Esther at six-years-old was a roamer. She was the most difficult to control. There were certainly enough chores around the home to keep her busy, but she was tough to keep track of. Generally it was easier for Rose to just get the job done than it was to get Esther in the mood.

At four-years-old, Tamara was a helper. Too young to carry water, but old enough to keep the hut clean.

Three-year-old Stephanie was simply in the way. She loved chasing the lakou baby chicks which warranted a few tender whacks from Fabiola and the other lakou mama's. Funnier than the mama whacks were the mother hens chasing Stephanie.

Then there was two-year-old Riderson. He was still an infant. Running around without clothing, he was always in the dirt. Tamara and Esther never quite got done keeping him clean.

As Rose thought about her siblings, she couldn't help but smile, thinking about how much she loved them. They had all been through so much together. Losing their mother still brought pangs of pain to her. The smaller children didn't remember Mama and had no idea how much she was missed.

The two plus years had passed quickly since Mama died, but the hurt was still fresh. Rose had now experienced loss and didn't like it. She did everything she could to keep her siblings safe and close. She couldn't bear losing anyone else.

Chapter 7

The day dawned like any other day, too soon and too full. Before her younger siblings were up from their rice reed floor mats, Rose had already returned from the river with the first two buckets of water.

Papa would need water to help wash the children when they got up and they would all need water for their morning breakfast. Rose set out leftover rice and beans along with a few plantains from last night's meal. The meager fare would have to suffice.

The children were growing older and seven mouths to feed was a never-ending chore. There never seemed to be enough food to feed the family. Rose worried as she saw Stephanie's hair beginning to turn a shadowy shade of orange. She was likewise anxious as she noticed both Riderson and Stephanie's stomachs growing larger. They both complained about stomach aches. She knew the stomachs weren't getting larger because of having too much to eat, as that would be a rare thing in rural Haiti.

Yet, this was another day, a special day. Rose knew it was her ninth birthday. None of her siblings mentioned it, and why would they? There was no calendar in the hut and days simply followed days. She wondered if her papa would remember.

Late in the afternoon, she saw him coming in the distance. He had a small sack in his hand. As he got closer her expectations rose, as he gave her a hug and the bag. She opened it to find beans and rice waiting to be cooked for their evening meal. She smiled and headed to the charcoal cooking fire.

Later that evening when they were alone outside the hut, he reached in his pocket and gave Rose a spool of ribbon. It was the most beautiful blue she'd ever seen! He used his knife to cut a piece for her. He gathered her black hair into a ponytail at the back of her head and tied a beautiful bow. Rose was excited.

Not having a mirror in their hut, she knew tomorrow she'd go to Fabiola's hut as early as possible to see how she looked. She was amazed her papa had remembered her birthday with all that was keeping him busy in life.

It had been a great day for Rose! But again, there was the shadow of what tomorrow or the next days would bring. The future was weighing on her in the same way mud clung to her feet at the riverbank.

~

Marie ran into the hut and bumped into Rose.

Rose, who was busy folding and stacking the few pieces of family clothing said, "What's the hurry?"

"Papa's coming and there's a man with him."

It was odd that her papa was coming home at mid-day.

"Who is it? Do you know him?"

"No, I've never seen him before."

Rose looked out the huts glassless window with a glance down the path. Across the lakou she could see her dad approaching. The other man was about her dad's age and was carrying two bags.

When they arrived, Moise told Rose and Marie they had a guest for the noon meal.

He said, "Rose and Marie, I want you to meet a new friend of mine. His name is James."

The other children were soon standing in front of their hut and were introduced to their guest.

Papa gave the two bags to Rose and said, "James brought us some food. Rose, will you cook it for our meal?"

Rose took the two bags into the hut. Opening one of them, she found a bag of rice, another bag of beans, eight mangoes, and something heavy wrapped in paper. She unwrapped it to find a large chunk of ready-to-cook goat meat!

She opened the second bag and saw bananas, tomatoes and avocados. At the bottom of the sack were two smaller bags. She opened one and found a pile of ribbons and barrettes for girl's hair and a small toy car.

The other small bag held a pile of chiclet chewing gum and hard candy which was covered in a colorful variety of bright crinkly wrappers.

Never in Rose's life had she seen such a cache of good things! She was overwhelmed at the treasure in these two bags. Wow, they were going to eat well today! If this had happened yesterday, she would have thought it was for her birthday.

Rose busied herself preparing the goat, rice and beans, while wondering who this generous man was. She made a tomato based gravy for the meal. She couldn't remember the last time they as a family had goat, or any meat for that matter, with their rice and beans.

She glanced over to see Papa and James talking to the other children and having a good time. Rose didn't mind doing the cooking. After all, she had been doing it for nearly three years and it was simply her chore to do.

The outdoor cooking area had tin sides and a canvas top to keep the rain out during the two rainy seasons they had each year.

The charcoal smoke from the cooking fire curled upward, hit the canvas and swirled back down. Rose coughed. She wished there was a way the smoke could get away instead of choking her half to death.

Though Haiti at one time was heavily forested, centuries of cutting trees for charcoal created a landscape that was now 70% de-forested. To make charcoal, men cut down the trees, chopped them into small pieces of wood about the size of a child's fist and then buried them in a large pit in the ground. Small channels for air-tubes were built throughout the pile of wood. The charcoal was lit on fire and then covered with dirt. The wood continued to simmer and was eventually cooled to produce charred wood or charcoal.

Charcoal is the primary fuel for rural Haiti for cooking. Sadly, the smoke is a significant accomplice in the respiratory issues many women and children have.

Coughing, Rose backed away from the outdoor cooking kitchen. Then she went back to cover the goat to let it simmer a bit longer.

Marie had gone to the river and had just returned with two buckets of water. She retrieved the cups and plates from the hut and placed them on a towel on the ground outside the home.

They had collected a number of plates, cups, saucers, forks and spoons over the years to accommodate all of them plus the guest. Though there were cracks and chips in the dinnerware and a fork or two had missing tines, they were ready to eat.

Papa had collected some pieces of fallen, palm tree trunks since the last hurricane and spread them out in front of their hut. Lying on the ground they had become their parlor chairs.

Papa invited his guest to take a plate and sit down. Rose brought the rice and beans to him. He ladled out a healthy supply onto his plate. The plate was the most beautiful one they had. It had a large picture of flowers on it. Though there were spider web cracks running through the bouquet, it was still the most beautiful plate Rose had ever seen.

James took a few pieces of goat and then spooned the tomato gravy on top. Alongside his rice and beans he filled in with avocado and mango pieces. He seemed pleased.

Papa followed suit, as did the rest of the children. Rose made sure each had plenty. Not until she had brought seconds to Papa and James did she sit down to enjoy some of what was left.

Marie began laughing as she watched little Stephanie eating her meat. With her clenched fist, she was holding the hairs on one side of her large piece of goat, and eating the meat and fat from the other side. Marie said, "As tightly as she's holding her goat, I don't think it'll run away!"

It took a while for Rose, Marie and Esther to clean up the dishes, pots, pans and utensils. Sitting on the ground, they used water from the bucket and a few flakes of soap to get the job done. Soap was a commodity they couldn't afford much of. A bar of soap would be used for their personal bathing and a knife would flake off a few pieces to use for dishwashing. They finished the pots, pans and dishes and put them away. It had been a feast they would all remember for a long time.

Rose told her papa, "I won't forget this meal. I can't believe our family has received these gifts from James. Who is he?"

"Let's all sit down and enjoy some candy."

James let each of the children select a piece of the colorfully wrapped sweets.

Papa said to each of them, "Suck on it. It'll last a long time. If you chew it, it'll be gone quickly."

It was the first candy most of them had ever had.

Rose said, "Papa, you haven't told us how you met James."

"Ah, you're right. This morning I was waiting in the village with other men for work. I had my shovel and hammer and was hoping for a digging or carpenter job. Several men were selected, but I wasn't. Then, this stranger James came up to me. He said he had a small business just up the road and needed help. He asked me about my family so I told him about all of you and how we missed your mama. I told him about our hard life. He seemed interested in hiring me. Since it was already about noon, he said I could start in a few days with the job, but first he wanted to meet my family."

Rose looked at James. He was smiling and lowered his head as the story continued. He seemed embarrassed.

Moise continued the story. "James felt sorry for our family and said he'd like to visit with all of you and help in some small way. So, that's why he's here today."

Moise looked at James and said, "Is there anything you'd like to say to my children?"

James looked up and smiled. "Many years ago, my mama told me of a Haitian proverb. *'When one member of a family suffers, the others will also suffer.'* When my mother died, I knew sadness and loss. My brothers, sisters and I knew what suffering was like. It was a very difficult life. I was unable to go to school and had no mother growing up. Most times, we didn't have enough to eat. My papa worked very hard, but it seemed we never escaped the difficult times. But, life has been good to me and I have a business. I'm glad I can share some of my success now with others. When your papa told me of your suffering, I decided to visit and see if I could help. Thank you very much for treating me so kindly today. As the saying tells us, *'Neighborhood is family'*, and I feel my neighborhood now stretches to your lakou."

Each of the children thanked James for what he had brought. Papa walked with him to the end of the path and they talked for a while longer, then Papa returned.

Rose said, "Papa, he seems like a really nice man. Is he your friend?"

"Yes, I think he's my new friend. Even more than that, he told me he could use me every day for work. He's now my boss. That means our family will have more food and money. I'm thinking today has been a very good day for all of us."

The rest of the day continued until dusk. Without electricity it generally meant it was time to prepare for bed. Candles were a commodity not easily available to the poor of rural Haiti. Darkness meant bed-time. So, Rose and Marie laid the small mats on the floor of the hut for the other four children. They were soon off to sleep.

Papa said to Rose and Marie, "Do you want to go to the beach?"

Rose looked overhead and noticed the moon was bright and full. There would be plenty of light to follow the path and she looked forward to time on 'her' beach with her papa and sister. She poked her head in the door and saw the younger children were sleeping. She smiled as she thought about her role as a nine-year-old mama. She loved her family.

They walked to the beach, careful to not step on broken glass. Fortunately the full moon cast shadows and reflected off the glass shards to prevent a cut on a bare foot.

Papa found a palm tree frond and smoothed off an area of sand for them to sit. With a sneaky smile, he pulled three pieces of wrapped candy from his pocket and passed them to his oldest daughters. Quickly unwrapped, all three were soon sucking the sweet luxury.

Sugar cane stalks were normally the only sweet thing they had to chew and suck on. It was the 'poor man's candy.' Unfortunately, over time, chewing on the bristly sugarcane wore down the teeth. This candy that James brought certainly was easier to suck on than the cane.

Marie said, "This day has made me very happy. I can't remember a better day than this."

Rose said, "Marie, you're going to make Papa feel sad by saying that. You're saying a stranger can bring us better days than Papa can bring."

"I'm sorry Papa. I didn't mean it the way it sounded. I only meant it has been a special day."

"I knew what you meant Marie. Life has been hard and it's important to receive good things with thankfulness. I'm glad you're happy. Since Mama died, we haven't had very many really good days."

Rose said, "That's true, but Mama always said, 'When you have family, you have what's important.'"

Papa said, "Thanks for the reminder. Your mama was a wise and thankful woman. We all miss her."

He paused and continued, "I do have something new to share with you. James brought us many gifts today. There was the goat, rice, beans, bananas, avocados, mangoes, toys and candy for a start. Then he gave me the gift of a new job. He also gave me a bonus, some money that will help us."

Rose said, "He must really feel badly for us. Maybe his past life taught him a lot about how to help others."

Papa said, "I think that's true. He's a good man."

Marie asked, "What does he get out of this? A heart that feels good?"

"I think that's also true, but he wants to help our family even more."

"How?"

"He said he would like to make life easier for one of my children. He would like to send one of you to school with his children."

Rose and Marie looked at one another.

"But if he gave you a job and a bonus of money, can't you send us to school?"

"Well, the job and money will help us with food today and tomorrow, but not enough to send even one of you to school in the future. Maybe over time I can save enough from my job to send Riderson. You know how important it is for a boy to be educated so he can raise his family someday?"

Again, Rose and Marie looked at each other.

Rose asked, "What are you thinking Papa? Is it good to accept all of this from him?"

"I don't think there's any other way. If one of you would live with his family..."

Rose quickly interrupted, "You mean one of us would have to leave this family and stay with his family?"

"Yes, he wants to help. He has three children and they're all going to school. One of you would be like his own child. Of course, you'd still be mine and we could always visit, but you would have the benefit of living with a family who has much more to share than we do."

Rose once again felt the growing shadow. A premonition. A pending darkness starting to settle in. She looked up and knew the shadow wasn't from the moon.

"So, who are you thinking would stay with his family, Rose or me?" Marie asked.

"James watched our family today when he was here. He saw how Rose was a leader and the oldest. He noticed how you taught Marie all the things you were doing. He was very impressed with both of you."

Moise said, "I hardly know what to think. I've seen the sadness in your faces as you talk about the other children in the lakou going to school. I see the orange hair happening in my younger children. I know my children have worms eating the food in their stomachs. I see how hard you both work. I don't see much changing in the future unless something changes now. I think this opportunity is something Rose should take advantage of."

Marie said, "But that means I'll need to take over all the work and Rose will go to school. That doesn't seem very fair."

"I think there are more families like James out there who would be willing to take another child into their home. I think your time will come Marie."

A lone tear trickled down Rose's cheek. It glistened in the moonlight. Moise noticed.

"What's the matter Rose?"

"One day at the river, right before Mama died, she pointed out the restaveks to me. They were children who had to leave their homes to live with another family because they were so poor. I saw the sadness in those children and saw how hard they worked. I don't think this is a good thing. He said he would treat me well and send me to school, but can we trust him?"

"Well, I just met him today, but he already has shown us a lot of kindness and compassion. Knowing his background, I think he feels our suffering. I think he's walked in our shoes."

Marie giggled, "We don't even have shoes, so how can he walk in them? If I had shoes, I don't think his big feet would fit anyway."

Papa continued, "I don't think we have a choice. This is an opportunity that's come our way without us even asking. Rose, I think you going to school will get you a job someday that can help our family."

Rose's uncertainty still showed on her face. Of course she wanted to help her family. Of course she wanted to be obedient to her father. Of course she knew her brother and sisters were suffering. Of course she wanted to make life easier for them. She knew ongoing poverty resulted in the early deaths of children and she certainly wanted to help prevent that. She loved her brother and sisters and would do anything to help them and save them from harm.

Rose said with tears in her eyes, "Papa, I can't even think of leaving our home and family. I shudder when I think about going somewhere new that's unfamiliar and strange. I've never been far from home, only to the river. Meeting new people makes me afraid. I don't know what they'll expect of me. What if they don't like me? What if they reject me? Can I succeed at school? I'm nine-years-old and will have to be in kindergarten with four-year-olds?"

She hesitated, then said, "Papa, if this is what you want me to do, I'll do it. For you. For my family, but only because I love you so much."

They sat a while longer, listening to the waves lapping at the shoreline and watching the moonlight glistening on the water. They were enjoying the time together as the future of Moise's family was being decided.

Then, with uncertainty, Rose asked, "When is this happening?"

Papa, looking at the ground, said, "Tomorrow at noon."

Rose felt a shiver go through her body. She knew she'd sleep little that night.

Chapter 8

Another dawn. Rose gradually opened her eyes. She laid on her mat realizing it had been a long night. There had been many thoughts running through her mind. In fact, she was ashamed to think she'd thought of running away in the middle of the night. She could have, but she had told her papa she'd obey him. She might have, but she had nowhere to go.

Now, the new day was here, along with the unknowns which would definitely change her life and that of her family. Papa was already outside getting breakfast ready. Rose was surprised to see he had brought two buckets of water from the river.

The other children began emerging from the hut. None of them other than Marie knew what this day held. Marie stole a glance at Rose and exchanged a sad smile. Deep inside, Marie was thankful she was going to remain with her family. But she had cried herself to sleep as she thought about her older sister leaving.

Rose remembered the emotions she'd had when her mama had died. Loss. Change. Grief. Sadness. She was sensing them all over again. Why was it all feeling like death?

Her spirits lifted when Riderson came to her and crawled into her lap. He said, "Good morning Rose."

She smiled at him and gave him a long squeezing hug. She'd miss this sweet little boy.

Moise watched them from the cooking area. He was feeling hopeful this morning and was excited for the opportunity Rose was being given. He knew her education and future work would provide a lot of hope to his family. It hadn't been an easy choice for him, but one less mouth to feed certainly left more food for the others. Some of his children were truly in a life or death situation.

He realized if nothing changed, he would lose one or two of his children to sickness and death. He had seen it a hundred times over the years. First would come the signs of lack of nutrition and food; then the ongoing cough and sickness; no taxi money, clinic or medicine; weakness; then death. Nothing changes if nothing changes.

He remembered the day he had been carrying two buckets of water up the steep path from the river and lost his footing. There was no stopping his freefall to a bone-jarring collision with the riverbed. Poverty had the same predictable kind of outcome. There was simply nothing to slow the inevitable conclusion of death.

They had a slow breakfast together. Moise told the rest of the children what was happening. There were tears. They had a time of remembering together as they reminisced about the past. Moise tried his best to explain how this wasn't the end of the world for them but the beginning of a good thing.

Rose did her best to put on a happy face. She didn't want to leave with all the children holding onto her and screaming.

Rose went into the hut and retrieved a small bag of her few things. A comb, barrettes, two pieces of hard candy, and a sliver of a mirror she had found on the beach yesterday. Also tucked away in the bag was a light green blouse that had belonged to her mama. In reality, it was the most precious possession she had.

They waited in front of the hut. Tamara said, "Here comes James!"

They all watched as James and a woman came down the path. He was with a beautiful lady wearing a bright yellow dress and carrying a large bag. The couple seemed so out-of-place in their lakou. Rose wondered how much her new life was going to change her.

James smiled as he came closer. He shook hands with Moise and then with each of the children. Then he introduced his wife, Marie Lucie. She went around the circle and shook the hands of everyone and gave them each a kiss on the cheek. When she got to Rose, she stopped and said, "Your papa and mama gave you the perfect name. You are a beautiful Rose. We're looking forward to having you in our family and our children are anxious to meet you." She gave her a kiss on both cheeks and hugged her.

She reached in her bag and pulled out some things for Moise and his children. More food, clothing and fruit.

Then she reached in the bag and gently held up a beautiful red dress in front of Rose. She said, "Go put it on. Let's see how you look."

Rose took the dress into the hut and came out a couple minutes later. Moise said, "Rose, you truly are your mother's daughter. You're beautiful! You really look like a rose in that dress!"

Rose was embarrassed by the attention, but silently appreciated it. Rose thanked James and Marie Lucie for the dress.

Moise took Rose to the side and said, "Rose, never forget our family. We love you and we'll miss you very much. You've been obedient by going with James and Marie Lucie and we'll never forget that. I think you're saving the lives of some of your sisters. We'll visit one another often. Do your best. You are my first born and your mama would be very proud of you today."

He placed two short stalks of sugarcane in her bag and said, "Here's a little something extra for you. I hope when you taste the sweetness of it later, you'll remember that is just how I remember you. My sweet little red Rose."

Rose held back her tears as she held, hugged and kissed her papa.

Then it was time to say goodbye to her sisters and little brother. Marie was last and only said, "I'll miss you very much. I love you."

The three walked the lakou path together. James on one side, Marie Lucie in the yellow dress on the other, and nine-year-old Rose in her red dress in the middle. Rose turned her head for another look at her hut, her lakou and her family, then the trio disappeared around a bend in the trail.

Chapter 9

As James, Marie Lucie and Rose emerged from the trail, they stepped up onto a small dirt road that wasn't much more than a motorcycle path. They walked for a few minutes. Rose knew this small road as it led to the river where she got water every day for as long as she could remember. With sweet memories, she remembered walking this same path with her mama and with Marie in the past.

Before they arrived at the river, James turned left onto another trail which they walked for ten minutes or so. Rose heard the noise of cars, trucks and motorcycles before she saw them. She had been here before, but no further.

At the main road, she saw a large mango tree and many huts along both sides of the road. As she looked at the tree, she remembered sitting under it a few times with Marie, watching the traffic coming and going. They had talked together as to what was at the end of the road in either direction. They had a great time trying to imagine life outside their lakou. This place, right here, right now was as big as Rose's world had ever been.

James and Marie Lucie walked with Rose to a car parked alongside the road and got in. Already, Rose was making new experiences and filled with awe.

The car began moving on the highway. The fastest she had ever moved was running down a dirt path. Her breath was almost taken away as they drove down the road. Sometimes James would pass slower cars, motorcycles or trucks. Sometimes, honking their horn, a car would pass them.

All the while, Rose was watching people. This was a very different life from her lakou. It was like she was in a different part of the world. Part of her was loving it while another part scared her.

James stopped the car. He and Marie Lucie talked in a language she didn't understand. She was surprised Haitian people could talk a language other than Creole.

After they were finished talking, Marie Lucie got out of the car, opened Rose's door and said, "Come with me." Rose emerged and held her hand.

Marie Lucie said, "You and I will be going in a different car. James will be going in another direction."

There was another car parked alongside the road which they got into. Now, Rose was in the front seat with Marie Lucie.

Rose was so fascinated with what she was seeing out the front window and where they were going, that she failed to watch where they had come from. She had wanted to memorize the way back to her lakou.

Marie Lucie told Rose how to close her window. She pointed to a small button on the door and asked her to push it. The window went up. She did it again and it came down. Finally, she left it up. The inside of the car began to get hot when Marie Lucie reached for a knob and turned it. Suddenly there was cold air coming into the car! Rose sat in awe. She had witnessed another miracle! She thought, *how life would have been different in our hot little hut if we could have done that!*

They began talking about things they were seeing outside. Marie Lucie pointed out the window and said, "I grew up in mountains like that."

Rose looked out the window to her right to see mountains and asked, "Are those the mountains you came from?"

"No, the mountains I came from are more in the north and east. I lived near the Dominican Republic."

"What do you mean, the Dominican Republic? Is that a village?"

Marie Lucie laughed and said, "Rose, your world is going to get bigger and bigger. The Dominican Republic is another country attached to Haiti. We share the same island."

Rose asked, "What's an island?"

"It means our land is surrounded by water."

"Does that mean no one can ever leave?"

"Oh no, I've left many times. We fly in airplanes or jets."

"What's an airplane?"

That started a conversation which went on for over two hours. Rose's eyes got large and her jaw dropped many times during those miles.

Rose was amazed at the mountains, the many, many people walking on the side of the roads, the piles of large bags of charcoal being hauled on the gigantic trucks, the small motorcycles carrying three and four people.

She had laughed out loud when she saw a man, his wife, a child and a goat riding on one motorcycle. She held her hand to her mouth when they passed a huge transport truck loaded to the brim with products, yet on the very top were fifteen or so people holding on. They weren't scared. They seemed to be enjoying the view and tropical wind in their faces.

They stopped for a toilet break and got something to eat at a roadside stand. The stand was just like her hut's outdoor kitchen. Marie Lucie bought rice, beans and goat. She also purchased a small plastic bag of water. Marie Lucie showed her how to bite off the corner of the bag to be able to drink from it.

Continuing on the main highway for another fifteen minutes, Marie Lucie turned off onto a smaller road. The road they took wasn't as wide and smooth as the one they left but it was at least paved. After another thirty minutes she turned onto another road which was made of dirt. Fifteen minutes later, she stopped.

Rose asked, "Where are we?"

Marie Lucie said, "We're in a small village called Carice du Sud. I want to introduce you to someone. A friend of mine lives here."

They stepped out into the bright sunshine. Right away, Rose missed the cool air they had felt in the car. It was much hotter here than where she had lived. She wondered how close they were to the sea and beach.

~

As she slowly started walking, Marie Lucie gently held her hand. The lakou they walked through was larger than her papa's by the sea. Rose did feel safe with her, though the experience of new things and new places was unsettling.

Rose's world had expanded dramatically in the last four hours since they had left her family. She was concerned for not having any idea where she was, or more importantly where her family was.

Passing a few ramshackle huts, they approached a nicer and larger home than she had ever seen before. There was no thatch on the roof or rusty tin anywhere to be seen. Rather, it was a squared-off home with a plastered finish which was painted a beautiful yellow and green. The roof was flat and Rose noticed a few chairs on top. At one side of the home, she saw concrete steps going to the roof. She saw a dog chained to the railing on the steps. There was a doll and a few toy cars lying on the concrete porch at the front of the home. On the other side of the home was a rope strung between trees with many colorful articles of clothing, obviously trying desperately to dry in the hot, humid and still air.

The carved front door was made of a beautiful wood with a metal knob. Marie Lucie paused and knocked. The noise almost echoed in the quietness. After a few seconds, the knob turned and the door slowly opened. A boy, older than Rose, smiled and welcomed them into the home.

Rose hadn't seen anything like this before. The floor wasn't dirt! Rather, it was covered by square tiles with brown and yellow mosaic designs. There were obviously more rooms than just the one they were standing in. There were multiple pieces of furniture including a couch and several plump chairs. Where did they eat? There was no kitchen table or chairs. Where did they sleep, as there were no beds?

The home smelled of bread and Rose realized she hadn't eaten for a while. Hunger wasn't new to her but the bread was smelling wonderful!

Within a minute a short, plump woman entered the room. She had a sweet smile and friendly face.

Marie Lucie said, "Ah, Farah, it's so good to see you again!"

They greeted each other with kisses on both cheeks.

Rose was surprised to hear the voices echo in this room of tile and concrete. There were no echoes in a thatched hut.

Farah said with a smile, "And who do you have here?"

Marie Lucie said, "This is Rose." She continued, "Rose, why don't you sit here in this chair while Farah and I talk about old times."

Marie Lucie and Farah went outside.

Rose was amazed at how cool the home was in spite of the heat outside. This home was certainly different than her own had been, in many ways.

Relaxing in the chair, Rose felt the material. It was clean and soft. The chair was so soft, she wondered if she could even get out of it. She had sunk into its depths. She thought it would make a great bed!

Then her mind wandered to her family. She wondered if Marie had gotten enough water for the family and whether she had started their evening meal. She hoped Marie was taking good care of Riderson, and that she hadn't forgotten to... then she smiled. She realized the responsibility of her family was no longer on her shoulders. Part of her felt free and excited, and then the guilt came. Why should I be the one experiencing these wonderful new things while Marie is now working so hard?

She heard other noises in the house and realized there were others here than just the boy and Farah.

As the minutes passed, Rose wondered how soon they would be getting back on the road. She knew the sun would be setting within an hour or so.

Several more minutes passed. Then Rose heard a car engine starting. As she listened, the noise of the car began to disappear.

The front door opened. Farah entered the home holding the solitary bag Rose had brought from her home. She crossed the room and dropped the bag in Rose's lap and said, "Come with me."

Rose peered past the wide Farah and searched the yard for Marie Lucie and her car. Again she heard, "Rose, come with me!"

Rose pushed herself out of the chair and followed Farah outside. They walked behind the house to a small hut. This hut was smaller than her papa's by the sea. This one had a tin roof with boards on the sides. Alongside the hut was a cooking area. Farah opened the door of the unpainted hut and Rose saw a dirt floor and a piece of tin on the ground. An old chair with a few pieces of clothing piled on it sat forlornly in a corner.

Farah said, "Rose, this is your place to stay. You aren't to leave it unless I tell you to. You'll be working for us."

Then Farah said, "Take off that red dress. You can't work in that. There's clothing on the chair for you to put on."

Rose reluctantly took the dress off and placed it on the chair. Farah grabbed it and held it while Rose put on a shirt and shorts.

Farah walked out clutching Rose's red dress. The door slammed shut. Rose heard a rattling of something metal. She watched through a crack in the wood as Farah walked to the big house.

There was something about Farah which prevented Rose from asking a question. Right now, Rose was full of questions. She felt a gripping fear she had never felt before in her nine-year-old life.

Then, she remembered the promises James and Marie Lucie had made to her papa and to her. Rose was having a very difficult time of making sense of those promises and what was happening right here and right now.

She remembered the question she had asked her mama at the river. "Will I become a restavek?" She also remembered her mama's quick answer, "No, no, no!"

They'd been riding in the car for several hours so Rose was hopeless in knowing which direction or how far away her own family was. Their quiet and familiar lakou and village had no name, so she couldn't even ask anyone about it.

Chapter 10

Remembering the clanking metal sound, Rose peered through one of the cracks in the dilapidated wood siding to see what had made the unfamiliar noise. There was a large metal lock on the ramshackle door.

Rose sat stiffly on the lumpy tin sheet on the ground and slowly looked around. There were no windows. There was a metal pot on the ground which she assumed was her toilet. There was nothing else to be found other than the broken chair in the corner.

The late afternoon sunshine was carefully sneaking into her space through gaps between the wood pieces making up the side walls. The sun's rays were also snaking through old nail holes in the rusty tin roof.

Rose stood. She walked from one side to the other. Three paces. She walked from the front to the back. Three paces.

The smell in the hut was nothing like the bread she had smelled in the big house. She raised her nose into the air and took a whiff. The odor was foul. She remembered a smell like it from another place, another time. She had been running through someone's lakou and her foot had stepped into a hole filled with rotting vegetables, fruit and who knows what else. She had run to the sea to wash the black garbage from her leg and foot. It had smelled just like this.

She heard someone coming. She looked out of a crack to see the young boy coming with a pan. Rose backed away from the door and stood at the back of the hut.

The metal lock rattled and the door opened. The boy looked inside and said, "Mama told me to bring this pan of water to you."

"What's it for?"

Laughing, he said, "Ah, you might be just as stupid as our goat. It's to drink!"

Embarrassed, Rose fell silent. Finally she risked a question. "What's your name?"

"Simon."

With that short introduction, Simon shut the door, rattled the lock and ran to the big house.

Rose greedily drank. It had been a long and physically tiring day. She wondered how long it would be before she'd be able to ask questions and get some answers. Sitting on the tin, the questions began to flood her mind.

Where am I?

Which direction is home?

Where are James and Marie Lucie?

When will I meet their family?

Why did they leave me here?

How are Papa and Marie doing without me?

When she thought of her family, Rose began to cry. The first tears fell quietly. Then as she thought of where she was and the uncertainty of what was ahead, in desperation she began to weep.

Suddenly, a loud banging began on the side of the hut. The noise echoed around the hut, bouncing off the tin and wood. Her sobs stopped, but her heaving shoulders didn't.

Farah's voice filled the shanty, "If you don't stop crying like a baby, I'll whip you until there aren't any more tears!"

Rose froze. She was fearful the door would open and the stout Farah would carry through with her threat. But nothing more was said.

Rose heard noises coming through the wall at the side of the hut where the cooking area was located. She heard the sounds of pots and pans.

Soon, the smell and smoke of heated charcoal seeped through the cracks in the wall where bright sunshine had earlier been shining through. She coughed and moved to the other side of the small hut, as if three paces would let her escape this misery.

Rose sat quietly as the family's supper was being prepared. After an hour or so, all was quiet as she watched Farah and a young girl carry the meal to the big house. She smelled the cooked plantains, rice and beans and some kind of cooked meat.

The smell of the food gradually was pushed away by the insistent returning smell of rotting garbage.

She knew her family back home was probably laughing and eating right now without her. Were they missing her?

Rose was really hungry. Thinking about her family eating without her stirred yet even more hunger. Though her family hadn't had much to eat, at least there were mangoes and bananas to fill their stomachs in the lean times. Oh, how she wished she had a mango and a banana! She had taken so much for granted in the past. What was that old saying her mama had told her? Then she remembered, *'You don't miss the water until the well runs dry.'*

~

Many miles away, Papa was saying, "This is our first big meal without Rose. Marie, you did a really good job in making it. I think your mama did a good job of teaching Rose and Rose did a good job of teaching you."

He continued, "Esther, I think it'll be good for you to learn some things from Marie. You're old enough now to learn about cooking."

Tamara asked, "What do you think Rose is doing right now? Do you think she misses us?"

Marie quickly said, "Of course she misses us. Look at us. How could she not miss this family of beautiful people?"

They laughed as they wondered what Rose was doing.

Papa said, "I'd think she's enjoying a wonderful meal with James and his family right now."

Marie said, "She's learning the names of his children and their ages. It's like she's getting a new family. I'd imagine they couldn't be as smart or beautiful as our family!"

Esther smiled and said, "With school tomorrow, I think they're giving her a backpack, books and pencils. She'll need those things for her classes."

Tamara said, "Today, someone at the river asked me where Rose was. When I told her what had happened, she said, 'I think Rose just found heaven.'"

Looking down, Papa picked up a handful of dirt and said, "I don't think heaven has dirt floors, paths or roads. I heard it has golden streets. I doubt any of us will find heaven here."

Rose's family laughed as the sun set behind a brilliant amber, red and orange sky.

~

At the same time, Rose noticed the yellow sunshine seeping through the cracks in the wall was now turning orange, then red and gradually the hut was getting darker.

She heard a noise outside the back of the hut and heard what she knew were rats. Obviously the constant meal of garbage was a bit of heaven for the local rat population.

Her papa had taught her a lot of things. She hadn't been to school, nor had he, but there was no end to what he was able to teach. He even knew about rats.

He had shared one evening, "Rats are ugly, but they love family. They'll protect each other to the point of sacrificing their own needs for one of their own."

Rose had responded, "That sounds like lakou."

"Yes, that is just like lakou. Maybe rats have been watching and learning from Haitians," he had said with a laugh.

"If you listen carefully to rats, you can learn their language. They hiss, squeak, chatter, and grind their teeth. When you hear the hiss and squeaks, they're usually afraid. When you hear something like chattering, they're actually grinding their teeth together. Their teeth grow all the time so they need to wear them down."

Rose had told her papa, "Rats scare me. I'm afraid they'll bite me when I'm sleeping."

He said, "I've heard of people getting bitten by rats, but it's a rare thing. You don't need to worry. Rats are usually busy feasting on garbage. That can make them your friend."

As Rose continued to hear the noisy rats, she relaxed. The good thing was, at least she wasn't alone.

The evening sun had set and the hut was dismally dark. Realizing she'd be going to bed hungry, she wished she had something soft to lay on. The corrugated tin would make a hard, lumpy bed tonight. She wondered if she should try to sleep on the broken chair.

Then she heard a door open at the big house. The tied dog barked. Someone was coming to the hut. There was a rattle of the metal lock. The door opened. A candle lit up the face of Farah and a young girl.

Without a word, Farah handed a blanket and a plate to Rose. They left. The lock clicked into place.

Ah, food and a blanket were like a gift from heaven. Rose smiled. Unable to see what was on the chipped and partially broken plate, she hungrily ate the rice, beans and plantains. It wasn't much but it helped ease her hunger. Maybe she could get to sleep tonight.

She thought about placing the cracked plate on the ground near the door but decided it would be better off the ground to keep from attracting more rats. She stood on the chair and placed the plate on the wood crosspiece holding the tin to the roof.

Rose placed the blanket on the tin sheet which was on the ground and laid on top. It was still hard and lumpy due to the ridges of the tin sheet, so she scraped dirt into the corrugations. She thought to herself that she had just practiced 'degaje' or 'making do' which her papa had taught her. She smiled.

Satisfied that the valleys and mountain tops of the tin were now level, she stretched out the blanket and laid down.

Realizing she needed the toilet, she got back up to use the metal pot in the hut. She assumed it had been placed there for that purpose.

Lying back down on the tin, she remembered something her papa had said, "Haiti received its name because of the mountains. There's no end to the valleys and mountains in our country."

Again, Rose smiled and thought, *this tin is just like Haiti. All valleys and mountains.*

As she looked up at the tin roof, she felt utterly alone. She could see no moonlight seeping through the nail holes. Since her eyes couldn't see anything of her surroundings, she concentrated on the sounds.

The night brought sounds similar to what she had heard at home. Dogs barking. A donkey braying. A goat bleating. A rooster crowing. Rose had learned roosters crowed all day and all night. There seemed to always be a rooster expressing himself.

If the roosters crowed and the dogs barked simply to hear themselves, that would be one thing. But it seemed they did it to let other dogs and roosters know they existed. Their crow or bark usually set off a noisy din of crowing or barking around the lakou and beyond.

It wasn't long before Rose could identify approximately where the other dogs were in the lakou. She could tell if they were young or old, full of energy or tired. She heard one young dog yapping and remembered an old saying from her papa. *'A little dog is really brave in front of his master's house.'*

Rose thought she must be like that little dog, but she wasn't feeling brave at all. If she were safe and secure in her papa's hut and lakou, she might be feeling brave. But here, there was no security or safety, only the unknown of the future.

She drifted off to sleep.

Suddenly, she was jolted awake by something which hit her on her shoulder. Jumping up, she had no idea what had happened. Her shoulder hurt, but feeling no wetness she knew she wasn't bleeding. There was no one else in the hut or she'd have been awakened by someone unlocking the door. She would have heard the door open with its creaks and groans.

Going back to her bed, her hands searched the ground trying to solve the mystery of what had hit her. She found the shattered remains of her food plate. Though cracked before, now it was in many pieces. A rat must have found it and dislodged it by trying to lick it clean. Rose wondered if rats were able to lick things since they had such large protruding teeth. In any case the mystery was solved.

Rose continued to search and found the various pieces of the plate and dropped them in a pile by the door. She laid down on her bed and was soon sleeping.

Chapter 11

The dawn entered her day on a slow crawl through a crack in the wall. As the light worked its way up the opposite wall, it reached Rose's face and she woke up.

When her eyes slowly opened, immediately the confusion hit her. This place, the bed, the tin roof didn't quite register in her memory. Then, suddenly she remembered. She didn't like what she was seeing, smelling or feeling.

At her papa's home she always awoke with familiarity as her companion. There, she knew exactly what another day would bring. She knew her chores and what to expect. Now, here in this place, there was nothing familiar. She knew dread for the first time in her young life. Worry became part of her and she was full of fear. Again, the questions came.

Why am I locked up?

Where are James and Marie Lucie?

What will be happening today?

As if in answer to her questions, she heard the door at the big house open and she heard the dog bark. Someone was coming. Farah...

The lock jiggled and the door creaked open.

Farah said, "Come out and bring your food plate with you."

Rose reached down and picked up the plate pieces.

Farah impatiently asked, "What are you doing?"

"The plate broke during the night so I'm picking up the pieces."

She said in astonishment, "Rose, you broke my plate."

"No, I didn't. It fell from the roof."

"Oh, now we have plates falling from the sky? That's a new thing in Haiti! I know an excuse when I hear one. You need to know you can never find an excuse good enough to cover your stupidity or disobedience."

"But, it was already chipped when I got it last night."

"That's another poor excuse. It sounds like you're quick to blame others for your mistakes. It looks like you aren't careful with other people's property. You need to learn."

"I wedged it into the rafter to discourage the rats from coming into my room. One of them must have knocked it loose. It fell and broke."

"I can't believe it. Plates falling from the sky! Rats breaking your plate!"

Farah grabbed her by the neck and marched her toward the back door of the big house. She took the broken pieces from Rose, threw them on the ground and said, "Stay here. I'll be right back."

Rose waited. Soon Farah came out the back door with an all too familiar tool in her hand. Rose had seen it often as she grew up. Those who kept cattle or goats used the rigoise to make them move. It was a twisted piece of hard leather about the size of Farah's little finger and about two feet long. A whip.

Rose had always felt sorry for the cows, donkeys or goats who felt the lash of the rigoise. But she had also been deeply angered to watch its use on children. One lash of the rigoise was enough to draw blood and leave a lifelong scar. It was a vicious tool.

When Rose or her sisters and brother had been disobedient, their papa had made them kneel on stones.

Sometimes he'd have them stand in the hot sunshine for a while. He had used his hand to discipline them a time or two, but never had he used a rigoise on them. He had said, "The rigoise whip is for animals and then only to be used on the very worst animal."

Yet, Farah was standing there with the rigoise.

Rose whimpered and moved away from the beady eyed Farah. Though Farah was short and heavy, her hands were undeniably fast. Rose was now in the firm grip of a strong hand.

Farah said, "Take off your shirt!"

Rose hesitated.

The shirt was yanked off and the rigoise was raised above Rose's back.

Rose screamed with the first blow. Crying, she raised her arm to deflect what was coming next. There were no more. Farah had stopped.

She said, "Rose, I'm trusting you'll learn with this one strike. I'm not afraid of using the rigoise on you again. You need to remember there are many more strikes hiding inside this whip. It's for animals, but until you can prove you're better than a dirty, stubborn, excuse-making donkey, it'll find a place on your back."

Rose cowered.

Farah said, "Put your shirt back on. You're too old to run around without your shirt."

Rose pulled the shirt over her head and moaned as the shirt drug across the broken and bleeding welt on her back.

Farah said, "You've taken something from me with the broken plate. In return I'm taking something from you. Bring me your bag."

Rose went to the hut, retrieved the bag containing the barrettes, broken mirror, comb and most importantly, her mama's light green blouse.

Farah grabbed the bag and said, "I hope this was a good lesson for you in how to care for other people's property. Most of these things will sell at the market."

She meekly followed Farah into the big house through the back door.

Chapter 12

Rose looked around the back room. The room itself was larger than her family's small hut. It was also much larger than her small hut by the garbage. Their hut by the sea had been home for her papa and six children. Rose wondered how many people lived in this huge home.

She saw a large wooden table with five chairs. On the wall were pictures of people Rose hadn't met yet. There was a cross on another wall and dishes in glass-fronted cupboards. There were liquor bottles on the counter and a large white metal box, bigger than Farah, standing upright along one wall.

Farah led Rose through the rest of the spacious house, one room at a time. There were three bedrooms. In the front of the home was the large room Rose had seen the day before with a large, soft sofa as well as three chairs. Along one wall was a table that had what looked like a large picture frame standing on it. It was then she heard a man talking. Looking at the frame, she was shocked to see a man moving and talking from the black glass. It was like a moving picture!

As Rose was looking around the room, the boy she had met at the door yesterday walked in the room. He was dressed in a school uniform and had a pack on his back. He watched Rose with a leer that caused shivers to run up and down her back.

Farah said, "Ricardo is twelve-years-old. You are to do whatever he and our other children ask of you."

Ricardo gave her a casual glance.

Then a girl and another young boy, also dressed similarly for school, came through the hallway.

Farah introduced them to Rose. "Nadia is nine-years-old and Simon is six-years-old."

They both smiled and then the three children disappeared out the front door.

Farah told Rose to sit on a chair and Farah dropped heavily into another.

Farah said, "I know you have questions. I have the answers. This will be the only time you'll get to ask questions, so make sure you ask everything you want to know."

Last night during the night, Rose had a hundred questions in her mind, but now she thought of only one.

"Where are James and Marie Lucie?"

"Ah, I knew that would be a question. Let me explain. James is a friend of ours from Port au Prince. He gets us things we can't find for ourselves here in this area."

She continued, "Marie Lucie works for James. I've known her for years. We went to school together and she introduced her boss James to us some years ago. She also lives in Port au Prince."

"But, James said he had a business and home close to ours by the beach?"

"Ha, did he? No, he doesn't have a business and home close to where you lived! He lives in Port au Prince."

Rose was struggling to make sense of what she was hearing. "He said Marie Lucie was his wife?"

"No, Marie Lucie isn't his wife. She works for him."

Now the questions were bubbling forward in her mind. "James said I could live with his family and he would send me to school along with his children. He would raise me like one of his own!"

"Well, that isn't going to happen, is it? He's a businessman and a successful one at that! He has a wife and children in Port."

"He told us about his life. He said he was raised without a mom and they were very poor. That was why he was helping us."

"Well, again, things are different than what James and Marie Lucie told you and your papa. He has never been a poor man and his mother is still living. I met her once in Port at his home. The only reason he's helping you is for the money we paid him to bring you to us."

"He was giving my papa a job."

"Your papa will be disappointed to know there's no job waiting for him."

The reality of what was happening began to settle on Rose like the heavy odor of garbage in her hut. As the truth began settling in, Rose quietly asked, "So, why am I here?"

Farah said, "I'm a busy woman with three very smart children. The work is too much for me to handle, so you'll be working for us. My children are busy learning and can't be bothered with chores."

Farah continued, "Do you have any more questions?"

"What will I be doing for you?"

"Everything."

"Who did this work before me?" Rose probed.

"That's no business of yours. But things can be different for you than what happened to the last girl."

"When will I be able to visit my family?"

"Rose, you won't visit your papa or your family. You won't have time for that with the work needing to be done here."

With the answer to that question, Rose finally understood what her life was going to be like.

"Will I be able to go to school?"

"Of course not. There's too much work for you to do." Then she paused, laughed and said, "I shouldn't have answered that question so fast. Yes, you'll be going to school. You'll be taking Simon nearly every day and then hurrying back here for your real work."

On the verge of tears, Rose asked, "How much will I be paid to do this work and how long will I be here?"

"Rose, you have a lot of questions. There won't be any gourdes going into your pocket. You'll get clothing, a place to stay and food in return for your work. You'll stay with us as long as we have work to do."

Farah continued, "Do you have any more questions?"

Rose's chin quivered. The thought of not seeing Papa, Marie, Esther, Tamara, Stephanie or little Riderson broke her heart. That was more of a blow than not going to school or working hard. It felt like the end of her world.

Rose said, "No."

Farah looked disappointed when Rose said 'no.' Rose thought Farah had actually enjoyed being the one delivering the bad news.

Farah said, "Now, I need to give you my rules. You've already learned there are many more welts left in my rigoise. Don't do anything to disappoint or anger me. Even more than that, don't do anything that'll disappoint or anger my husband or our children. If you do, there will be a price to pay and it's more than you can afford!"

She continued, "Today is the only day you've been allowed to ask questions. That won't happen again. In fact, you aren't permitted to speak to me, my husband or my children unless they ask you a question. We'll give you what you need to get your work done. You'll begin in the mornings and you won't quit until your work is finished. When you're in the market, at the water pump, or at the river, you aren't to speak to anyone. If you ever try to run away or try to get in touch with your family, there'll be trouble. You need to remember that James and Marie Lucie know your papa and your family. He makes a business of finding girls like you to help out other families. If you make trouble for our family, he'll make sure Marie or one of your other sisters becomes a restavek just like you. And, yes, I do know the names of your family. Now you know what I know and you know what I expect from you."

Taking Rose to the back of the house, Farah said, "Here's the room that has all your cleaning supplies. With the broom, bucket, mop, brush, rags and soap, you have what you need to keep our home spotless. Inside and outside."

Looking at the cleaning tools, Rose knew she was looking at her future and it was looking pretty dismal.

They went to the kitchen and stood in front of the white metal box with a handle. Farah pulled the handle and Rose felt cool air on her face.

"This is a refrigerator. We use it to keep our food cold and fresh." She shut the door.

"I'll tell you three times a week what food to purchase at the market. Some of the things you'll buy, like meat, will be stored in the refrigerator. Other things will be stored on the counter. I told James we needed a girl who could read and write. He failed to find me that girl, so we were able to pay him less for you. You're almost worthless to us, so you better pray your memory is good.

"You'll take Simon to primary school almost every morning and you'll bring him home at noon.

"It will be your responsibility to get water as often as we need it at the village well. Don't ever let us run out of water. You'll empty the pots we use in the house for our toilet. During the day we use the outdoor toilet, but in the evenings, rainy seasons and during the night our family uses pots.

"We have a generator to produce electricity for our lights and to keep the refrigerator cold. Our children need to study their school-work and watch television. It will be your responsibility to keep fuel in the generator."

Rose said, "What's a television and where do I get the fuel if we're out?"

Farah went to the cupboard and opened the door. She reached in, pulled out the rigoise and said, "Take off your shirt."

Rose quickly complied and received another wicked lash of the hardened and twisted leather. With a whimper and tears, she put her shirt back on quickly.

Farah said, "Well, you learned to quickly get your shirt on, but you forgot you aren't permitted to ask a question. Don't you remember what I said about never asking questions? I'll answer it this time. My husband Carlos will make sure there's fuel available. He has a truck and will bring what you need. Oh, a television is something you'd never understand so I won't bother answering that question."

She continued with the rules, "You're never permitted to come in the house except to work. I want you to have all your housework done during the day. You aren't to be in the house late in the afternoon or evening. You'll be making our evening meal at the outdoor kitchen area by your room."

With that being said, Farah motioned Rose to follow her outside to the front of the house. She showed her the area of the lakou yard she wanted swept. That alone seemed like a never-ending job. There were chickens pecking and running in the yard, dogs continually dragging things around, people dropping their wrappers and sacks and the wind bringing in the neighbors trash.

Farah showed Rose the generator at the back of the house. Opening the diesel fuel cap, she showed her where to put the fuel and how to start it and stop it.

The dog without a name needed to be fed and the chickens needed to be tended to. Though the chickens had their own fenced area for safety at night, they needed to be let out in the morning and chased into the pen in the evening. Farah showed her how to lure them by bribing them with corn.

They went into the back door to the kitchen once again. There, Farah pointed to the food scraps, fruit peelings and rinds in a bucket by the counter. Rose picked it up and Farah led her to a large hole in the ground directly behind Rose's 'bedroom.' Rose saw and smelled the garbage rotting in the hole and knew rats would be her long-term neighbors.

Farah took Rose back to the house and got her started on cleaning all the bedrooms.

"After you're done with the bedrooms, you can clean the floors in the living room and kitchen areas. You'll do these rooms every morning. After you're done with the rooms today, I'll inspect them. Then we'll see if the rigoise will have some of its own work to do."

Farah laughed at her own joke. Rose began to think Farah enjoyed having power and control over other people. She hoped Carlos would be kinder than his wife. She wondered what he would be like and knew he probably couldn't be worse.

Rose gathered her cleaning supplies and headed to the first bedroom. While sweeping the floor, she heard the sound of a truck and the resulting crunch of gravel near the home.

She didn't dare go to the door or window to see what was happening or who was coming. Rather, with her head down and looking at the floor of the bedroom, she swept. After sweeping and cleaning the room, she began collecting her supplies and was going to move on to the next bedroom.

She was startled by a man standing in the doorway watching her. She looked at the floor and waited. Finally, the man said, "I'm Carlos. You must be Rose..."

Rose didn't know if it was a statement or a question. If it was a statement, then she'd be in trouble by responding. If it was a question, she'd be in trouble if she didn't answer. So, she said nothing and looked at the floor. Fear of the rigoise over shadowed everything!

Carlos said, "I asked a question. Are you Rose?"

Rose quickly responded, "Yes, I'm Rose."

He took three quick steps and stopped a foot away from her and looked down at her. He put a finger under her chin and lifted her head so he could look into her eyes. He asked, "Why are you shaking Rose?"

Again, no answer. He asked again, "Why are you shaking?"

Rose said, "I'm... I'm afraid."

Carlos said, "Rose, you don't need to worry. I'll never hurt you."

Rose felt relief. The man seemed to be kind and gentle. Then she remembered James and realized not all things are as they seem. James had been the kindest man, other than her papa, she had ever met. Then she remembered that hadn't turned out so well. Rose was learning many lessons about trust in the last two days.

Carlos stepped back and walked around Rose. Finally he said, "I think you'll be a fine addition to our family."

Rose had no idea what that meant. Farah had made it very clear she'd be no part of this family and yet Carlos was saying she would be?

Carlos said, "We've been looking for a helper and it seems James has done a good job in finding you for our family. It's very difficult to find young, strong and pretty girls to do work. You'll do well, I think. I can't imagine the terrible place you've come from. It must have been very difficult living in such poor conditions. I'm thankful our family can save you from that horrible life."

With that, Carlos walked out the door. Rose picked up her supplies and went to the next bedroom. Walking through the door, the first thing she saw was her very own red dress hanging on the wall! It was Nadia's bedroom. Angrily she began sweeping. She casually looked around as she swept. There were books, lots of them. There were crayons, dolls, pictures on the wall and a bowl of candy. She noticed bottles of colored paint and guessed it was for fingernails. Rose had seen painted nails before and had no clue why anyone would want to do that. Paint was for houses.

The balance of the morning was spent in cleaning the rest of the rooms. She was amazed to see Ricardo and Simon's room. They certainly had 'stuff' she hadn't seen before. The room was filled with clothing, balls, shoes and books.

Rose thought she'd really like to have an extra hour to explore the items in the children's rooms but knew that would never happen!

~

Rose was confused. Farah had said she wanted to inspect the rooms after she was done cleaning. She wasn't permitted to speak to Farah nor could she ask a question. It was a guess as to how to approach her, so Rose began looking for her. She couldn't find her in the house, so she went out the front door and found Farah in a chair on the front porch with a large glass of tea. There were square pieces of what looked like glass floating on the top of the tea.

Rose stood by the door and waited.

Farah said, "What do you want?"

Ah, a question! Rose said, "I'm finished with the rooms. Do you want to inspect them?" Then horrified, Rose realized she had just asked Farah a question!

But Farah merely responded, "Yes, when I'm finished with my tea."

Rose continued to stand by the door until Farah said, "Why are you still standing there? Get busy sweeping the front lakou. There's trash and garbage all over out there. We don't want our neighbors to think we're poor or dirty people!"

Rose quickly retrieved a broom from the closet and began sweeping the dirt in the yard. She picked up the paper and other debris and put them in a bucket. The mid-day sun was hot. Perspiring, Rose had a glimpse of Farah nonchalantly watching Rose work. Farah was perspiring as much as Rose even though she was sitting in the shade, not working and drinking tea. For the first time in her life, Rose felt resentment.

Rose was hungry and thirsty. She realized she had not eaten anything since her rice and beans last evening. No breakfast? No noon lunch? She was going to waste away to nothing at this rate.

She kept sweeping.

Farah slowly arose from her soft cushioned porch chair and entered the home. Rose kept sweeping with an anxious eye on the front door. She knew Farah was inspecting her work in the various rooms. Rose was expecting Farah to emerge through the front door at any time with the rigoise.

One minute passed. Then two. Then three. Still no Farah. She continued sweeping.

Finally she could see no more trash, garbage or debris in the lakou so Rose took the bucket to the garbage pile and emptied it. Entering the back door, she placed the broom and bucket in the closet.

Pausing, she listened for an indication as to where Farah was. She heard nothing... or, was there something? She picked up a bucket and rag and went to the large room. The noise was louder. She cautiously entered the hallway. Tiptoeing forward, she looked in Carlos and Farah's bedroom to see Farah sleeping peacefully and snoring on her bed.

Just as quietly Rose went outside and began washing the front porch floor. Then she washed the porch chairs.

Finally Farah came outside and said, "Rose, my bed is messed up. Fix it."

She dutifully untucked the sheets, re-smoothed them and re-made the bed.

Nothing had been said by Farah as to whether the rooms were adequately cleaned. Rose hated this feeling of not knowing what was good, bad, acceptable or unacceptable. There was always the threat of the rigoise. The frustration of the unknown was horrible. At home, she could always ask questions of her papa to change unknowns into knowns. He was always willing to help her learn.

Her papa had asked her to do many things and she was always willing to do the chores or tasks because she loved him and her siblings so much. Now, she was asked to do the same things for Farah, but it was different. She was doing them out of fear. What a difference love made!

Farah hollered, "Rose, come here."

Startled and fearing the worst, Rose obeyed quickly.

"It's time to talk about washing clothing. In each bedroom is a basket of dirty clothes. Gather them and bring them to the back of the house."

Washing clothing wasn't a new thing to Rose. She'd had a few years of experience. In fact she enjoyed it. At her home the washing happened at the river. Absent-mindedly she wondered how far away her own river was. When she washed clothes in the past, the fun part was talking to the other girls who were also washing. That made it enjoyable.

Rose gathered the clothing and took the load to the back yard.

Farah said, "Get the large wash-pans from the back room and I'll get you started."

Rose retrieved them and laid them out on the ground. Rose didn't dare ask where the water was. She stood quietly until Farah said, "It's time to show you where the village well is."

Rose gathered two buckets and followed Farah down a path. They walked for two or three minutes past several other homes. None of the homes were equal to Farah's. The village homes were definitely more like Papa's home. Small, some with thatched walls, some with concrete walls and mostly with rusty tin roofs.

They arrived at the Carice village well which had a hand pump. There were a number of children surrounding it. Some with old plastic paint buckets and some with gallon plastic containers which had once held detergent or other liquids. When Farah arrived, the group parted like magic and Farah walked to the front of the line. Motioning Rose to follow, she said, "Rose, start filling your first bucket."

Rose complied. When full, she barely had the strength to carry it to the side. Knowing she couldn't carry two, Farah said, "Leave the second bucket here and carry the first to the house."

Rose immediately worried that someone would steal the second bucket if they left it. But as she saw the fear in the children's eyes when they saw Farah, she knew no one would dare take the bucket.

Rose began the slow and tortuous walk back. It took longer than the earlier two or three minutes. Some water spilled and Farah slapped the top of Rose's head. More carefully, Rose lugged the bucket to the back of the house.

Farah said, "Go fill the other bucket and bring it back."

Rose hurried to the pump. A boy, older than her was filling his bucket. There were four other children waiting in line. Rose got in line behind the last and waited.

An older girl in line said to Rose, "Farah's an evil woman. She doesn't hesitate to push or slap us when she comes for water. You better be sure you don't disobey that woman. She's hurt others and she could hurt you very badly."

She continued, "What's your name?"

Rose stared blankly at the girl and didn't respond. "Ah, Farah told you not to talk to anyone, has she? We know that woman like the back of our hand."

Again, Rose didn't respond.

"Well, I'm sad for you."

Rose saw the sadness in the girl's eyes.

Ten or so minutes later it was Roses turn. She filled her bucket and began her trek back to the home.

Farah met her in the back yard and said, "That took you a long time. Did you talk to anyone?"

With a trembling voice, Rose said, "No. No one."

"Well, you'll need to find a better time to go to the pump when less people are there. You've wasted fifteen minutes of my time that you could have been working for me. Figure it out."

Rose began washing the clothing.

Having returned from school, the children stood at the back door and watched for a few minutes as Rose washed their clothing. Each was eating a snack and drinking something out of a can. Rose didn't dare make eye contact.

Seeing them eat increased her hunger pains. She had been so busy she had forgotten she'd not eaten since last evening.

Finally finishing the wash, she hung the clothing on a rope strung between two trees. Placing the pans and buckets in the closet, she looked for Farah. Finding her in the large room at the front of the home, she awaited instructions.

Farah took her to the kitchen and showed her where the plates, cups and utensils were. She instructed her as to how to set the table for the evening meal.

Then they headed to the outdoor cooking area beside Farah's hut. Farah began cooking the evening meal and said, "Watch closely because this is the last evening meal I'll be cooking for my family. Beginning tomorrow afternoon, you'll cook the evening meal. Tomorrow morning I'll teach you how to cook breakfast and later in the morning, lunch. After tomorrow you'll do all the cooking."

She continued, "After my family eats our meal, you'll gather our plates, pots and pans and wash them. Then you'll put them away. After that's done, I'll give you your food for your evening meal."

They continued with the evening cooking for another thirty minutes or so, carried it to the kitchen and placed the food on the counter. Farah said, "Rose, you can go to your hut. I'll call you when I need you."

Rose walked into her hut and fell to the floor exhausted and very hungry. She had never been so hungry or so tired. She thought she may as well get some rest, so she closed her eyes for a second or so...

"Rose! Rose! I need you."

Startled, Rose awoke and wondered how long she'd slept. She ran to the back door and went into the kitchen. She began gathering the pots, pans, plates, utensils and carried them to the back yard wash pan. Gathering the scraps from the plates, she dropped them into the garbage pit.

After washing all the supper items, she put everything away in the closet and kitchen. Farah handed her a plate of rice, beans, plantains and a thin piece of bread. Rose eagerly took it.

Farah said, "Rose, I know I told you to never talk or ask questions. I'll change that. You're expected to say 'thank you' and 'I'm sorry' when it's appropriate."

Rose looked at the food and immediately said, "Thank you."

"Okay. I'm finished with you for tonight. I'll get you in the morning when I need you."

Rose hastily made a retreat to her hut. Though small and very inadequate, it was a quiet place. The only thing missing was family and love... and that was everything. She felt like someone without a home.

Farah arrived shortly and locked the door without a word.

The rice, beans, plantains and bread disappeared quickly.

Chapter 13

A rooster nearby abruptly woke her at dawn. Rose laid quietly on the thin blanket which covered the dirt and corrugated tin. She wondered what the day would bring. The work was incredibly difficult and seemed never-ending. However, that seemed small compared to the ever-present fear of disappointing Farah and getting the welt-producing end of the rigoise.

Soon, she heard the back door open and slam shut. She stood, smoothed her hair and picked up her plate.

Farah arrived at the door and unlocked it. She had seemed surprised to see Rose standing just inside the door with her plate in her hands.

"It's time to make breakfast. Let's see what you can do without me telling you."

Rose started the charcoal fire and arranged the rocks so the pot would fit neatly over the fire without tipping into it. She began to make a plantain soup. She let the liquid heat on the fire while she and Farah went to the kitchen.

She put the bowls and plates on the table and retrieved the bread from under the large plastic cover on the cupboard. She opened the refrigerator, relished the five seconds of cool air, grabbed the butter and placed it on the table.

At the cooking area, the soup was hot and ready to eat, so she carried the pot to the kitchen. The children ate their breakfast with their parents and left for school.

Breakfast and supper are small get-by meals in Haiti with the large meal being at mid-day. So, after breakfast they began preparing for the noon meal. Rose and Farah soon had four pots on the fire. One for rice, another for beans, a third for beef and a fourth with a tomato gravy. Cautious to keep them from getting too hot, Rose got the job done. At 1:00 the children came home from school, Carlos returned from who-knows-where and the family had their meal.

Farah told Rose, "Yesterday was an unusual day since Carlos wasn't here at noon. So we ate the big meal in the evening. Usually we'll eat when the children come home from school at 1:00."

Rose went to the outdoor cooking area and moved the charcoal around to let it die out. She then grabbed the broom and began sweeping debris from the front yard. Rose wondered where all this trash and paper came from. It seemed to never stop. Carlos came through the front door, got in his truck and left. Rose noticed he watched her work as he drove away.

She went to the kitchen, cleaned up the lunch debris, washed the dishes and put them away. Farah gave her a bowl of the plantain soup from breakfast and said, "Don't dawdle, you have work to do."

The afternoon was busy in going to the well twice, cleaning the front porch and the rest of the rooms in the house. She had gagged as she carried the pot of waste from Carlos' and Farah's room to dump into the outdoor toilet which was near the house. Rose couldn't understand why they couldn't go outside during the night. She made a mental note to carry the waste out in the morning when it was less smelly.

And then it was time for the evening meal preparations.

~

After the small evening meal was finished and cleaned up, Rose went back to her hut. Farah followed her there to lock the door, or so Rose thought. But, Farah said, "Rose, I have a question for you."

Rose waited.

"I've been locking your door at night. It's a waste of my time to always come here to lock you in and then unlock it in the mornings. We've told you we know your father's name, the names of your sisters and your brother, and where they all live. We've said if you're disobedient, you'll get the rigoise. But if you run away, you need to know we'll immediately go to your father's house and your family will lose their home. Your papa will get a horrible beating. If he's hurt and can't work, you know your brothers and sisters will become restaveks, just like you."

"So, if I leave this door unlocked, will you promise to stay here and not run away?"

Rose nodded her head and Farah said, "I need to hear you say it!"

Rose said, "I promise."

"You promise what?"

"I promise to stay here and not run away."

"Okay, I'll leave it unlocked." With that, Farah returned to the house.

Rose laid down on her dirt mattress.

Her mind began to relax and the inevitable and never-ending questions came.

What's my family doing right now?

Do they miss me like I miss them?

Do they know what's happening to me?

Will I ever see them again?

My days are so busy, I haven't even gone to the market.

How will I get it all done if I take Simon to school?

Then she was struck with horror. She realized the lock on the door kept her from leaving but it also kept everyone out. Terror gripped her throat just as surely as a tether around a goat's neck. Her heart raced as she suddenly felt extremely vulnerable with the door unlocked.

Rose was feeling incredibly insecure, unsafe and unloved. She was feeling helpless and hopeless. She was feeling despised and shunned. Just today at the well some of the children called her 'restavek' as if they were talking to a dog or a goat. She was beginning to think she was the lowest of the low.

Chapter 14

Rose's Family

On the day Rose had left, Moise's family tried to make the best of her absence, but Riderson didn't make it easy. He had missed his big sister from the very beginning. Rose had been Riderson's mama for almost three years, so all Riderson ever knew was Rose taking care of his needs. She was his mama.

Moise had a tough time getting him to stop crying that first night. It still wasn't easy.

The day after Rose left, Moise arose early and headed to the village. He sat and waited for James and the promised job. Employers came, hired other men and left. One of them had tried to hire him, but Moise told him, "No, I have a job I'm waiting for."

Moise continued his wait. At noon he wondered if he had misunderstood James. Finally as the day wore on, he headed home. James obviously hadn't meant today, probably tomorrow.

He arrived home with five children looking expectantly at his empty hands.

But the next day was no different. No James. No job. All he did get was a growing concern about Rose.

On the third day, he chose a different plan. He went to his bed, lifted the mat away from the wood and pulled several coins from a crack in the bed-frame. Pocketing a few gourdes, he headed out the door with a quick set of instructions to Esther and the other children.

He hurried down the path to the village. There he hollered at a motorcyclist taxi who turned around and came to Moise.

"Take me to Caracul du Sud."

Moise climbed on the back and fifteen minutes later hopped off at a village he'd never been to before.

Looking around, he saw a woman at the side of the road cooking food. He approached her and asked, "Where does James live?"

"James? What's his last name?"

Moise suddenly realized he didn't know James's last name. He said, "I don't know. Do you know a James?"

"Yes, there's a James who lives east of here." Pointing to a path, she said, "Follow that path to the large mango tree that has yellow paint on it. He lives in the big house."

James set off at a quick pace. He was anxious to see Rose, but then realized she would already be in school. He hurried anyway as he wanted to find out about his job.

As he saw the large mango tree in the distance, he saw a yellow and orange band of paint on the tree and knew he'd found his destination.

Approaching the front door, he knocked and waited. Soon a cook with a flour covered apron opened the door.

"Good morning. Can I talk to James?"

"What's it about?"

"It's about some work he wants me to do."

"Come in."

Moise entered the very nice home and felt out of place with his bare-feet and not-so-nice clothing. He was happy to see that Rose had such a beautiful place to live.

Soon, an elderly gentleman came into the room.

"How can I help you"?

"I'm looking for James of Caracul du Sud?"

"I'm James and I live in Caracul du Sud. What's your name and what is it you need from me."

"My name is Moise. I'm from west of here along the coast. A man named James said he lived in this village and would give me work. He and his wife took my daughter to live with them and said he would give her an education. He said he'd give me work. I have five other children and I need the money. You're not the James I'm looking for. Is there another?"

James's smile disappeared as he said, "Please sit down Moise."

Moise felt as if he'd come face to face with something horrible. He numbly sat down.

James said, "Moise, this isn't the first time I've heard of this other James. A girl from this village was taken from her family last year by a man named James. He was also going to give work to her papa."

Moise swallowed. He asked, "What are you saying? What can I do?"

"I'd encourage you to talk to that girl's family. Maybe they've learned something."

James gave Moise the directions. With a thank you, Moise hurried down the path. Finding the lakou, he found a mama with her baby sitting in front of a very poor hut.

"Are you Judith?"

"Yes."

"My name is Moise. Did you have a daughter who left a year ago with James?"

The mama stood up quickly with an anxious look on her face. "Yes! Did you find her?"

The concerned and fearful look on Judith's face along with the anxiousness in her voice was a bad omen to Moise.

"No, I don't know anything about your daughter. James and Marie Lucie took my daughter three days ago to live with them so Rose could go to school."

"That sounds like the same thing that happened to our Mirlande. It's been over a year since she left. We've not heard from her or from James and Marie Lucie since then. We knew something wasn't right and you bringing your story to us is the first we've heard anything. You and I both know there's not much poor people like us can do about things like this."

They blankly and helplessly looked at each other. What else could be said? There was nothing, other than a sinking feeling something bad was happening to their daughters.

Moise began his walk back to the main road. He had the coins to hire a motorcycle, but these coins needed to be saved for his children.

No job.

No Rose.

No hope.

He began the seven mile walk back, knowing the hours would give him time to determine what to tell his children.

Chapter 15

Jesulah

Jesulah was seven-years-old when she became a restavek. She was still living with the same family now, two years later, and those years hadn't been easy. She laid on her bed after a hard day's work and thought about her young life.

She thought about her mama and her two sisters. Her memories of her papa were faint and not good ones. In fact, she tried not to think about her papa when she was going to sleep because it would bring nightmares. But, sometimes the memories came anyway and she couldn't push them away, as hard as she tried.

She remembered the many times her papa had beaten her for no apparent reason, other than she just happened to be the one close by when the inclination struck him. The bad memories of her papa all involved beatings. She remembered in excruciating detail the horrible beatings he had given her, her sisters and her mama. It seemed to all be related to his alcohol consumption.

He bought local concoctions of liquor and sometimes squandered their family money for store bought alcohol. It seemed when he got drunk, which was often, the ladies of the house got the brunt of his anger.

Then suddenly, he was gone. Mama had said he had moved to Port au Prince for work. One day in the market, two years after he had left, a woman told Mama that Papa had a new family in Port au Prince.

Mama didn't seem to be overly concerned or even hurt when she heard it. Maybe she had assumed it would happen, as it happened often in rural families like hers. Maybe more accurately, she was simply glad he had left.

After Papa was gone, life became easier in some respects. But in other ways it became even more difficult for their little family. Though he had been abusive, at least he had brought home a few gourdes and food sporadically.

Tears filled Jesulah's eyes as she thought of what had happened on that fateful day two years ago. A tearful Mama had said, "I can't continue to raise all three of you girls." She went on to say that she wanted Jesulah to have an opportunity for school and a better life.

Mama had heard a woman say she knew of a family looking for someone like Jesulah to help them. Arrangements were made and Jesulah left her family for what seemed to be an answer to her mama's prayers.

Jesulah's absence probably did make life easier for her mama and two sisters with one less mouth to feed. But life certainly didn't get better for her. She was working very hard from dawn to dusk for the new family, but at least she had a bed and food. She was thankful for that.

She had recently seen another restavek girl at the village water pump and learned that life could be tougher. She had never seen a girl look as sad as this particular girl. The girl had ragged clothing, was thin and had hair beginning to turn orange. As Jesulah looked into the girl's eyes, it was like looking into emptiness. It haunted Jesulah.

Jesulah had said, "I haven't seen you before, what's your name?"

The girl merely looked at her and Jesulah wondered if she possibly couldn't talk.

Again, "What's your name?"

Nothing.

Jesulah walked away dumbfounded. In the following days, she saw the girl again and again. Finally, one day, the girl reluctantly and quietly spoke. Jesulah almost didn't hear her.

"My name is Rose. What's yours?"

That had begun a bond between them, though it was a strange friendship. Rose was always full of fear and looking over her shoulder. She had been told to never talk to anyone.

One day, Rose approached the village water pump limping. Jesulah asked, "What happened to you?"

Rose showed her a large red, bleeding welt on her leg.

"What happened?"

"I was late in getting the family's little boy to school and his mama whipped me with a rigoise."

Rose began to share a few things with Jesulah about what life was like for her. Jesulah began to feel more thankful about her own life. It could undoubtedly be worse.

Jesulah's heart broke for Rose.

~

For Rose, taking six-year-old Simon to school every day was both a good and a bad thing. She loved seeing all the children dressed in their school clothing and was amazed to see a hundred children at one time. It was a bright spot in Rose's day.

At the same time, it caused her to feel envious. She so wanted to be in school. She knew the world was a bigger place than the little spot she occupied and she knew she had no way of learning about the larger world. So, her envy and resentment grew in volume every school visit.

It didn't help to know that other restavek children were having a better life than she was having. She had met a girl her age named Jesulah who had shared the details of her life. Jesulah's life wasn't good, but it certainly was better than hers.

If Farah had found out Rose was talking to someone at the well or on the paths, the rigoise would have been busier than it was.

After Farah stopped locking the door to Rose's hut, Rose began to feel more comfortable and safe. She no longer felt like a prisoner. Even so, the unlocked door created a temptation for her every night. She continually pondered the possibility of running away. In her internal debate, she'd go through the usual questions and answers...

I can't run away because I promised Farah I wouldn't.

I can't run away because the rigoise would be used if I were caught.

I can't run away because Farah and Carlos would do horrible things to my papa and family.

If I ran away, maybe I could find a better family to live with.

If I ran away, maybe I could find my way back home.

I can't run away because I don't know anyone else other than Jesulah. Oh, maybe Jesulah's family would take me in!

The thoughts as usual came and went. Finally, Rose realized she was stuck in a horrible situation with no realistic solutions, other than being perfectly obedient to Farah.

Rose began her usual pre-sleeping ritual of thinking about her distant family. Her memories of them were there, but she could feel herself slipping and sliding into another world where those old memories were starting to fade. Months with Farah's family was taking a predictable toll on her beautiful memories of a previous life.

Finally, sleep came.

~

The next day, Rose wearily went to the village pump after taking Simon to school. She hated carrying water multiple times a day, every day, with no end in sight, but it was part of her new life. She noticed her lower left abdomen had a significant bulge and created pain when she carried the heavy buckets.

The one redeeming thing about carrying water was she was able to periodically talk to Jesulah. As she approached the well, she spotted her waiting in line.

Quietly, Rose said, "I'm really happy to see you. I don't know what I'd do if you weren't my friend."

"I'm glad you and I can talk. It seems we don't have much else happening in our lives. I think we help each other get through our tough times."

Then Jesulah said, "Rose, does your family go to church?"

"No. Does yours?"

"Yes. I hear them sometimes talking about it. The things they say cause me to think. I think church is one of the reasons my family treats me better than yours."

"Why do you say that?"

"They talk about a book and the things it says. I hear them talking about a Jesse and his teachings. Last night I overheard them talking about how people need to live by what they read in the book and by what Jesse taught." She paused, smiled and said, "Oh, I think the name was Jesus, not Jesse."

Rose said with a giggle, "I wonder what Jesus says about the rigoise."

Jesulah laughed and said, "I have no idea, but I do know the family I'm with doesn't ever beat me. I don't get to go to school or church, but at least I get enough to eat and they don't own a rigoise!"

"Why don't you go to church?"

"They said I need to stay home and fix their noon meal so it'll be ready when they come home after church."

"I wish we could go to church."

"I do too, but I doubt it'll ever happen."

Rose's face lit up with an idea, "What if you started your meal sooner? Do you think then they would let you go?"

"I could start it earlier and let it cook and simmer, but they still wouldn't let me go. I don't have the right kind of clothing. I think they'd be ashamed of me. I'm not like them or those who go to church with them."

"Maybe you could sit outside the church window and listen? If you could do that, then maybe you could learn for both of us."

They had been so busy talking they hadn't noticed everyone was gone. Hurriedly they both filled their buckets, hugged and rushed back to their homes.

Chapter 16

Rose

Silence. Exhaustion. Sleep. Then... a sound. Something a bit skewed and odd from the usual night noises. Rose opened her eyes. Her heart started to beat faster. The rat neighbors could be a noisy bunch, but this was different. Her unlocked door creaked open. Rose sat up with a stifling fear that wrapped its ugly fingers around her neck.

Then, she heard someone whisper, "Don't be afraid Rose. I'm not here to hurt you."

She recognized the deep voice of Carlos. She knew she couldn't speak or ask a question. She knew she could only answer questions which were asked of her.

Carlos carefully sat down next to her on the tin and said, "I know your life isn't easy here. I also know Farah can make things rough. She's my wife but she doesn't always want to hear what I have to say. She tells me the home is hers to manage and that you work for her."

He continued, "I wanted to tell you that I'm not like my wife."

With that, he stood up, walked to the door and left.

Rose had been shaking while he had been sitting beside her. She started to calm down as he disappeared in the moonlight. She thought about what he had said. He had seemed kind and understanding. She laid down and fell asleep.

The next morning all seemed normal. Farah was her usual gruff, unkind and demanding self. The children were distant and treated her with their usual indifference. Carlos got in his truck without a word or glance in Rose's direction. Things were normal.

Her day was predictably the same as the ones before. The usual chores were incessantly waiting to be checked off the ever-present list. She dutifully needed to take Simon to school, get water from the well, go to the market, empty and clean the toilet pots, do food preparations, scrub the pots, pans, plates and utensils, sweep the yard, clean the rooms and front porch, wash the clothes and bed linens and of course, try to stay out of Farah's way and line of sight.

The day had been full and the end of any day was always a welcome time.

~

For the second night in a row, Rose awoke to the same sound. Something was just a bit different than the normal night sounds. Then, the door opened. Tonight her heart didn't race as much as the previous night.

Carlos entered the hut and sat on the tin beside Rose. He said, "I didn't mean to scare you. Are you okay?"

Rose hesitated.

"It's okay to answer my questions."

"Yes, I'm okay."

"Good. I just wanted to let you know I appreciate you helping my family. You're doing a good job for us. We're poor so we can't pay you, but I do appreciate what you're doing. You're a very pretty and special young lady. I wanted you to know that."

Rose didn't respond.

Carlos put his arm around her tiny almost ten-year-old shoulders. He put his other hand on her outstretched leg.

Rose shuddered.

Abruptly, Carlos stood up and said, "Good night Rose. I'll see you again."

Chapter 17

Jesulah

It was Sunday morning. Jesulah decided to get the noon meal started early for the family she stayed with. No one asked her any questions, so she hurried through her other chores and kept the pots hot and cooking. The family had left and she quickly headed down the path to the village church. Her heart was beating fast, not due to hurrying, but rather fearful of being caught.

Halfway there she remembered she hadn't covered the pots and pans cooking on the charcoal. What if a dog ate the lunch? Struck with horror, she ran back to the home and was relieved to find everything intact. Putting lids on the pots and readjusting the charcoal she took a peek at the rice, beans and beef which were simmering. Everything was looking and smelling really good. She put rocks on top of the lids and headed down the path once again.

She heard the peaceful singing before she saw the small concrete block church. The church had openings for windows, but no glass. The large wooden doors were wide open. The three concrete steps and open door looked very inviting, but she knew she had to remain hidden.

Her heart melted as she heard the wonderful harmony coming from the sixty or so men, women and children. The singing was loud and beautiful. She could pick out the voices of the children singing and wished she could be a part of it.

She approached the side of the church and sat under an open window and listened. She shut her eyes and imagined being inside in a white dress, with bows in her braids, sandals on her feet, a Bible and songbook in her hands. She imagined sitting with family and feeling included, safe and happy.

Then, opening her eyes she looked at her dirty bare feet. She looked at the ragged shorts she was wearing and the patched sleeveless top. Reality set in. She was an unwelcome outsider, a restavek, a nobody.

Then the pastor began reading from the book. Listening intently, she heard him speak of the man Jesus. He was reading about how Jesus taught his twelve friends the things they should and should not do. Jesulah, with a smile, soaked it up like a thirsty sponge.

After twenty minutes or so, she quietly slinked away from the window and headed down the path. The singing started again and she was glad to capture it in her heart and mind. She had just made some sweet memories.

Arriving home, she found the food safe and just about ready for the family. She was glad Rose had thought of this idea. She knew she'd be doing this again and again. She looked forward to sharing what she heard with Rose the next day at the village water pump.

Chapter 18

Jean Pierre

Jean Pierre had been a small six-year-old when he became a restavek. At first he couldn't bear the horrible loss of his family. He grieved nearly every night with tears for the first year. Gradually the memories of his family started to dim. He tried desperately to hold onto the fading memories and the emotions attached to them, but his feeble attempts were futile. They slipped and slithered away, little by little.

There had been three boys in his family as well as two sisters. He was in the middle of the children. Living in Port au Prince, his dad had work as a laborer in the market. He made his living by pulling a wooden cart full of produce, fruit, meat, car batteries, tires or whatever else needed transported within the market. The pay wasn't great, but Papa provided for his family. The Haitian gourde coins accumulated slowly and surely.

The oldest two children were in school and Papa had said Jean Pierre could go next year. He was excited!

The family was close and his mama and papa showed the children abundant amounts of love and care. There seemed to be nothing more important to them than their children.

Almost three million people lived in the Port au Prince metropolitan area. That meant nearly a third of all Haitians in the country lived in or close to the capital.

It was the dream of many rural Haitians to move to Port and find the job that was just waiting for them. Many dreams were shattered as the uneducated poor farmers found city life incredibly difficult and jobs nearly impossible to find.

But Jean Pierre's family was among the fortunate. Papa had a job and his children could eventually go to school. There was enough to eat and Mama was a great cook. Jean Pierre knew life could have been more difficult.

Papa and Mama had moved to Port when they married almost fifteen years earlier. Their extended families lived somewhere in the southwest. Jean Pierre and his family had visited their village a year ago and found things would have been worse for them if they had lived there. Again, he felt fortunate.

Jean Pierre's home was situated on the steep mountainside overlooking the capital city. There were thousands of homes tiered up the slope. They were so tightly packed it almost looked like one roof from a distance. But intertwined between the homes were dirt paths, rocky trails and small crowded streets.

Though some memories had disappeared for Jean Pierre, some would never leave. He would have liked to lose some memories, but they were part of him. Sometimes the memories woke him in the middle of the night as nightmares.

The reoccurring nightmare had its roots deeply embedded in the horror and tragedy of one horrible Tuesday afternoon on January 12, 2010.

It was 4:53 p.m. and he had been playing in the street with a friend. They had been kicking a homemade soccer ball back and forth. Jean Pierre's older brother had stuffed rags and plastic bags tightly in a cloth sack and tied it with string. That resultant soccer ball worked well for two boys who were intent on kicking it to an early death. It was nearing its old-age death with colored and muddied pieces of sack and rag leaking out between the string wraps. The boys had to be careful where they kicked the ball. The downward slope of the mountain would have carried the ball farther down to another happy boy's open hands.

Jean Pierre had just kicked the ball to his friend when something unexplainable happened. He felt a jolt and almost before he knew what happened, he was flat on the ground. The jolt threw him down with a slam. He couldn't comprehend. It didn't register with anything he had stored in his memory bank. It was like a dream. Things were happening that just didn't quite make sense.

After the initial jolt, the ground began shaking violently. He started hearing a low rumble which continued to build in intensity until it sounded like a solid roar. It was like a monster had just woke up from a long, deep sleep.

As the noise increased, dust began to swirl and soon Jean Pierre was choking and coughing, desperately trying to get his next breath.

He tried to stand but the violent shaking of the ground knocked him down again. Finally he was able to get on his knees.

Out of nowhere, something slammed into his leg and something hit him on his head. He tried to raise his hand to his head, but immediately fell flat on his face again.

Jean Pierre laid on the ground shaken by the tremors and the sheer terror running through his body. He tried to get a glimpse of what was happening, but the dust was so thick he couldn't see anything around him.

The shaking lasted for almost a minute. For a moment then, things were quiet. Then, a new noise began to come to his ears. He began to hear screaming and moaning. He stood up on shaking legs since the tremors had ceased. He looked around and still couldn't see anything due to the grey veil of dust.

He slowly began shuffling to where his friend had been. He looked down and saw him on the ground covered with a grey and white grimy dust.

He got on his knees beside him and said, "Lamy!"

No response.

Jean Pierre began shaking his friend... then he stopped. He saw red liquid mixing with the white dust next to Lamy's head. A large chunk of concrete had hit him and he knew his best friend was gone.

As he sat in the street next to Lamy, he heard a few car alarms blaring. There was the indescribable and incessant moaning and screaming. Then he heard what could only be described as a howling coming from around him. He knew things would be getting worse before they got better.

After several minutes the dust began to settle enough so he could begin to see the devastation surrounding him. Then, suddenly he remembered his family!

He looked for his home. He didn't recognize anything. What had been huts and homes in his neighborhood were now crumbled jagged piles of concrete, wood, tin and steel. Small pieces of concrete littered what had once been his street. Larger pieces with twisted steel rebar sticking out of it were strewn everywhere.

Large slabs of concrete were resting at an angle on top of what had been homes. Then he realized the slabs had once been roofs for those homes. Massive chunks of concrete and steel were everywhere, nestled in place where homes once stood.

The moans, groans and screams were coming from under some of the slabs of jumbled concrete. Jean Pierre knew people were trapped and suffering from injuries. The howling he was hearing, he now knew was coming from mamas, papas, children and neighbors as they realized the devastation of their homes and more significantly the loss of those they loved.

Then, somehow, someway, he knew which tangled mass of rubble was his home. He then remembered his older two brothers and dad had gone to the market. He remembered his mom and two sisters had been in their home, washing clothes and preparing their family's supper.

He began to run, but fell to the ground. He looked at his leg and saw blood coming from a large cut above his right knee. Then he remembered his leg being struck by something. That reminded him that something had also hit him in the head. He reached to the side of his head and winced as he felt a gash in his scalp. He brought his hand down and looked at it. It was bright red.

Though injured and in pain, he went to where he knew his house had been.

Jean Pierre screamed at the top of his voice, "Mama! Mama! Mama!"

He paused and then yelled, "Madeline!"

Nothing.

"Samantha!"

Nothing.

With a growing and gnawing feeling of terror, he began stepping across chunks of concrete and rock. Hollering for his family, he kept searching.

He noticed some familiar items in the rubble, so he knew he was at the right home. Distractedly, he listened and watched, as across the street, someone shrieked. In a daze, he saw a man holding a limp child in his arms.

Frantically, Jean Pierre dug at the rocks and rebar with his small six-year-old hands. They began bleeding. Then he stopped as he saw something black. Reaching down to what he thought was a rug, he touched what he immediately knew was hair. He pushed rubble, dust and blocks away to expose what he soon found to be Samantha's hair. He knew she was gone and he also knew he couldn't dig her body out.

His wails joined the howling he had been hearing. He continued searching but found nothing of his mama and Madeline. The concrete roof of their home had collapsed entirely into their home.

Jean Pierre, now in shock went to the street and sat. Silently, he looked out over Haiti's capital city. All he saw was a demolished Port au Prince. There was still a dusty shroud over the city. The sun was setting but was invisible through the dust. Here and there he saw smoke from fires. The earthquake happened during the late afternoon as many evening meals were being prepared. In the chaos, the charcoal fires spread onto nearby paper and cloth and created sporadic blazes.

The screaming and moaning hadn't subsided. It had only grown louder and louder. The mournful wailing came from every direction.

Then, a vicious jolt! And again, another round of violent shaking and earth tremors. Jean Pierre was horrified. How could this be happening again! Would it ever stop? After half a minute, all was quiet again, but just for a barely noticeable moment. Then the screaming, moaning and wailing started all over again.

He sat in the street and watched as a naked man walked toward him. The man was almost entirely covered in grey and white dust. There were streaks of dark skin showing below his eyes and down his cheeks where tears had probably washed away the dusty grime. There were also strips of brown skin showing where streaks of blood were flowing down his legs. He slowly walked past Jean Pierre, not glancing to the right or left. He looked like a zombie risen from the dead.

The man across the street had lain his distorted, limp child on a slab of concrete. He was now silent as he stood guard over his only son.

A woman and child ambled down the street. She said, "Help me, help me, help me. I don't know what to do. I don't know where to go. I can't find the rest of my family. Where is God?" Her voice trailed off as she continued down the concrete strewn street.

Jean Pierre got up and went back to the front of what had been their home. Again, he hollered, "Mama. Mama. Madeline."

No answer.

He no longer called Samantha's name.

Alone and helpless, he went back to the grey, rubble strewn street and sat down. He looked at his leg and realized the dust and grime had slowed down the bleeding. He reached up and felt the gash in his scalp and noticed there was no new blood. He tried to hold the flesh together with a blood stained and torn hand.

He sat and waited.

Another jolt... another round of tremors. Each time the after-shocks happened, the terror started all over.

He continued to sit and wait. Where was Papa and his two older brothers? They'd know what to do.

Darkness had come only two hours after the earthquake. Sitting alone in the dark was terrifying. There were fires across the city. Every now and then there was an explosion, sparks and more fire. Jean Pierre didn't know what hell looked like but it couldn't be much different than this.

Sitting in the dark he was afraid his papa and brothers would return and he wouldn't be able to see them. So, periodically, he would mournfully call out into the darkness, "Papa... Papa... Papa..."

No answer.

It was a long night. Several times the after-shocks returned and woke him from a frightful sleep.

As dawn arrived, the new day in Port au Prince, Haiti began. Jean Pierre opened his eyes to a new and devastated country. Things would forever be changed. It was now a world full of destruction, loss, pain, hunger and unknowns. His leg and his head were hurting. Then he remembered finding Samantha. He had a growing sense his mama and Madeline were also crushed under the roof. He began thinking his papa and brothers weren't going to return.

He wept as only a six-year-old child can weep when finding themselves suddenly and tragically alone in a world of ruin.

He decided to walk down the street to find someone or something familiar. Along the street were bodies laid neatly like cordwood. Old, young, babies. Some were missing arms or legs. Many had open and bloody wounds. He was seeing things no child should ever see. These were the things which would bring nightmares later.

Another tremor. He was almost getting used to them. They were a part of his new world. The terror still rose in his trembling body, but they didn't plunge him into shock any longer.

Two men carrying a door with an injured woman on it passed by him. A woman was erratically running down the street, angrily screaming, "My God, my God, my God, where are you?"

Walking past another large home that had been crushed by its plunging concrete roof, he saw a group of men working. Some of them with shovels, some with picks and some using their hands to remove rubble. He stopped to watch, next to a growing group of weary and bedraggled people.

Someone said aloud, "I think they saw the arm of someone buried in there."

Suddenly a man said, "I saw a hand move!"

Frantically but carefully, they continued moving blocks of concrete to uncover a man. He was still alive as they pulled him from what ultimately was going to be his coffin and grave. This man wouldn't be joining the row of Haitians lying like cordwood along the street!

Jean Pierre smiled for a brief second or two and then clapped his hands along with the others watching. Then he remembered his family.

He sat on the street and cried.

Chapter 19

Jesulah

The day after eavesdropping at the village church, Jesulah waited for Rose at the water pump. She was as antsy as a chicken waiting for cracked corn. She couldn't wait to tell her how Rose's idea had worked and what she had heard from the pastor.

When Jesulah thought she couldn't wait any longer, Rose came down the path and smiled at her.

Jesulah quickly said, "Rose, your idea about getting my Sunday meal ready earlier worked out really well. I was able to listen for about twenty minutes yesterday. The singing was beautiful. As the pastor talked I thought this is how school must be. Sitting and learning. It was great!"

Rose said, "I'm really glad to hear it went well for you. I wish the same plan could work for me. I think I'll have to hear all about the book and Jesus from you." She smiled and said, "You can be my eavesdropper and messenger."

As Jesulah pumped water into Rose's bucket she said, "The pastor was talking about Jesus. He said he was God's son and he came to deal with the evil things men and women do. Since those things are so horrible and God hates those wicked things so much, God demands payment for them. He said men and women can't be good enough to please God by themselves no matter how hard they try."

Rose's mind soaked it up as she asked, "So how are men and women supposed to pay for it?"

"Oh, they can't. He said there isn't enough money in the world to cover that high of a price. The exciting thing was that

God said if His Son Jesus would die for those evil men and women, it would be the only payment that would work."

"Why would a father let his son die for bad people? Believe me, I know some really bad people and there's no way I'd die for them! I also know my papa would never, ever have given me away to die."

The moment Rose said those words, she realized her papa had given her away. Well, at least she knew the circumstances were different, or so she thought.

Jesulah continued, "The pastor read something out of the book that said, "God loved the people in the world so much He gave His only son Jesus to die for them. If they believed in Him, then they wouldn't ever have to die, but could live in Heaven forever."

"Never die?"

"Well, there was something else he said about their bodies dying, but their soul could go to Heaven."

"Their soul? I don't understand that."

"Well, I don't have all the answers. I was only there for twenty minutes, remember?"

Rose laughed and said, "Yes, I remember."

Jesulah said, "It sounds like the most important part is whether or not we believe in Jesus and learn how to follow Him."

It was Rose's turn to fill her second bucket and Jesulah headed home after a quick hug and smile.

Chapter 20

Jean Pierre

When Jean Pierre saw the buried man rescued from the crumbled home, he went to the group of men who had carefully dug him out.

He said, "Can you help me? My mama and two sisters are in my home."

A man looked down at him and asked, "Where are they?"

Jean Pierre pointed up the street.

"Are they alive?"

"I don't know about Mama and Madeline. I know Samantha isn't."

"Let's go. Show us your house."

He led the men quickly up the narrow, rubble-strewn street. All were armed with shovels and picks as they threaded their way to his house.

Expectantly, he said, "This is it. I'll show you where my sister is."

Stepping over the concrete ruins, he took them to where he had found Samantha.

Disappointedly, he said, "I can't find her. I know she was right here but now the spot is covered with more rocks and concrete."

The men looked at one another until a large man with a shovel said, "The aftershocks from the earthquake are causing more and more concrete to fall. It looks like that's what happened here. Let's listen if we can hear anyone."

The group began calling for his mama and Madeline. No answer. They paused and listened intently, but again, no answer.

Then suddenly a man said, "I think I heard something!"

He called again. They listened.

There was a weak but audible, "Help me!"

The men moved closer and closer to the sound. They were careful to not dislodge the concrete pieces or to crush whoever was underneath.

No one was visible, but again, a faint sound.

The men began frantically removing the blocks and rubble. Soon they saw an arm. Finally they saw a face covered with dust. One of the men said, "Hold on Madame, we'll have you out soon. Your son led us to you."

The weak voice said, "I don't have a son."

Jean Pierre looked past the men at the woman and saw his neighbor, Fredeline.

"Fredeline, where is my mama and Madeline?"

The men pushed Jean Pierre out of the way, as again with hope they continued to dig to free the woman from her trap. She had been entombed for a night and a day. They saw how fortunate she had been to have an open space around her head and upper body created by falling concrete. The space gave her room to breathe. Most people weren't that fortunate.

Quickly they got her free and carried her to the road and gently laid her down. There were cuts and dried blood on her arms and leg. Her leg was so twisted, they knew it was broken. But she was alive.

Again, Jean Pierre pressed in and asked, "Where's my mama and Madeline?"

Fredeline looked up at him and said weakly, "I'm sorry Jean Pierre. Your mama, Madeline and Samantha were crushed in the kitchen by the roof. I had been there with them. I was just leaving and almost out the door of your house when the quake began. I just about made it out. I'm so sorry. Your mama and two sisters are gone."

Jean Pierre crumpled onto the dusty street, surrounded by a group of men who paused, but were ready to move on to the next home and potential survivor.

He sat alone in the street and cried.

Chapter 21

Rose

Rose laid on her lumpy bed of corrugated tin, dirt and thin blanket and wondered what her family was doing. Were they missing her? She knew Marie would be doing a good job of caring for her family, but even so, Rose hoped she was missed at least a little.

As she was thinking about her last night on the beach with Papa and Marie, she heard a familiar noise in the back yard. The door of her hut creaked open. Even in the dark she recognized the silhouette of Carlos.

He whispered, "Rose, it's me again."

He sat beside Rose on the tin and said, "Are you doing okay?"

Rose answered his question, "I'm okay."

"Good." His arm slid around her shoulders once again.

She shuddered.

"I wanted to make sure you were all right." His other hand rested on her leg.

Rose shuddered again as his right hand touched her chest and his left hand inched up her leg.

Then a noise. The hut door creaked. Carlos quickly stood up as Farah entered the hut with a dim flashlight.

She snapped, "Carlos, what's going on in here?"

Carlos immediately said, "Rose asked me to come and visit her. I don't know what she wants. I was just about ready to find out."

Farah looked at Carlos, then at Rose. "Rose, I've told you not to talk to anyone."

Rose said, "Madame, I..."

Farah slapped her as hard as she could across her face. "You're not to talk to anyone, including me or Carlos. I've told you that!"

Rose teared up and the tears flowed down her face, but there was no whimper.

"What did you want to talk to my husband about?"

Rose kept quiet.

Another slap. "Rose, I've told you that you're to answer questions. What did you want to talk to Carlos about?"

"Nothing."

"Nothing! That's not what Carlos said."

Another slap. "That's for lying to me!"

Carlos said, "She tried to touch me. I think she's trying to win me over so I'd do her favors."

Petrified, Rose stood quietly, not believing how Carlos was throwing her to Farah, the wild dog.

Farah walked out of the hut and went in the back door of the big house. Within seconds she was walking back to the hut with the rigoise. The way Farah was slapping it in her hand, Rose knew blood would be spilled this evening.

Farah ripped the shirt off Rose and threw her to the ground. She began lashing Rose again and again. Rose wailed. Farah was breathing hard. Rose was hoping she'd soon run out of breath and have to quit her whipping frenzy.

Farah stopped. She paused as she caught her breath. She started to turn away but paused again. Turning around she delivered a hard kick to Rose's exposed side.

With a snarl she said to Carlos, "Get rid of her."

Rose was terrified and in pain. Her mind raced. Her breaths were short. Her side had a sharp pain and her welted bleeding back was on fire. Her eyes darted left, then right, as she looked for a way to escape. She knew she'd soon be cut into small pieces and dropped in the garbage pit for her rat neighbors. She waited.

Carlos said, "What do you want me to do with her?"

"Tomorrow you need to call James or Marie Lucie and tell them they owe us a restavek replacement. Tell them the new girl had better be a good one this time and not a liar."

Rose was relieved she was still alive. She was hoping she could go home, but that seemed to be impossible. Maybe the new family she'd be sold to would treat her better than Farah's. She thought it couldn't get any worse!

~

The next morning it was work as usual for Rose. The only difference was the horrible pain in her side from the kick and the burning pain from the many lashes on her back.

Rose knew by the end of the day something would be changing. Maybe James would send her back to her papa. That was a sweet thought which helped her get through the day. She'd have a lot of stories to tell her family!

Last night as Farah had headed to the house she told Rose about an ancient proverb. *"'When you give a blow, they forget – when you leave marks, they remember.'* I think you'll remember this night!"

She wondered if anyone would tell the authorities about Farah's actions. Then she realized no authority would ever listen to what Rose's friends had to say. Her papa used to say,

'Money is the key to the door for a rich man, but there are no keys for the poor.'

The day wore on. In the late afternoon, Carlos arrived in his pick-up. Getting out, he walked to the house without a glimpse at Rose who was sweeping the yard.

Five minutes later James and Marie Lucie arrived. They likewise didn't bother looking at Rose. Rose wondered how many times she herself had walked past a mangy goat or worthless dog without looking at it. She was sure these people considered her a useless animal as well.

James, Marie Lucie and Carlos came out the front door. They talked but Rose couldn't hear their muffled whispers. Finished with sweeping the yard, she headed around the side of the house only to be stopped by Carlos saying, "Rose, come here."

Rose turned around and stood alone, ten feet from the group. She was trembling with her head hanging.

James said, "Carlos and Farah don't want you as their houseguest any longer. Get your things."

Rose almost laughed when she heard the word 'houseguest.' Dutifully, she went to the hut, looked around one last time and went back to the front yard empty handed.

"Get in the car."

She opened the back door and crawled in. Shutting the door, she waited.

Soon, James and Marie Lucie opened their doors. Almost immediately Marie Lucie scrunched her nose and said, "Rose, you stink worse than a goat! Don't you ever take a bath?"

James said, "We'll stop at the river."

Minutes later, they arrived at the river. Marie Lucie said, "Go and wash yourself. All over!"

Rose walked toward the river and moved upstream until James yelled, "That's far enough. Hurry, we need to go!"

Rose remembered the sweet time with her mama bathing at the river. It seemed so long ago and brought bittersweet memories of another time and another place. Then as she headed for her bath, she remembered a Haitian proverb her papa had shared, *'Smelling good is expensive.'* He had said only the rich could afford soap and perfume. This river would have to suffice.

James and Marie Lucie sat down under a mango tree watching Rose enter the river. James picked up a rock and tried to knock down a ripe mango. He was good at it and soon had three in his hands. Taking out a knife he peeled one for Marie Lucie and one for himself. Rose wondered, but not for very long, if the third was for her.

At first the water hurt her torn back, but soon the cool water softened the dried blood. Gradually she was able to get clean, or at least cleaner than she had been. Putting her clothing on, she returned to the couple under the mango tree.

James said, "Rose, I told you if you cause problems we would do some bad things to your family. We're going to give you another chance. We have another girl for Carlos and Farah so they're going to be okay. Fortunately there's a man named Wilson close by who needs a helper. We'll go there now."

He continued, "Don't forget, this is your last chance. One more problem and your papa and your family will pay a price. I know you don't want that!"

Chapter 22

Jean Pierre

Jean Pierre picked himself up from the street. He had been waiting almost three days for his papa to come home. He had dutifully stayed in front of his house waiting. But the smell coming from the rubble had begun already on the first day and it was getting worse and worse. Even when he walked down the street in either direction to get away from the smell, the stench of rotting flesh was the same. There was no way the many bodies buried under the rubble could be retrieved without heavy equipment.

Everywhere he looked, there were corpses lying in the street and no one was coming to remove them. He had overheard men talking about the deep ditches being dug to bury the bodies in, but he'd not seen any of them. The smell everywhere seemed to stick in his nose. There was no escape from it.

He had searched and searched for food in many of the crushed homes to no avail. His only food had been bread given to him by an old woman his mother had known. She seemed to pity him. He knew she didn't have enough for herself and certainly not enough for him.

Fortunately it had rained a little and he was able to drink from a few places where the water hadn't been able to evaporate or escape.

He noticed more and more people were leaving his street. Some had balanced baskets full of their belongings on their heads, others were carrying over-stuffed suitcases. All were walking and all looked sad and distracted.

He noticed there were many children like him wandering the streets. All looked dirty, dazed, sad, lonely and hungry. Jean Pierre wondered how wide this devastation was and how many people were hurt or killed. Already he had counted 138 corpses lying on the street near his home.

Jean Pierre decided it was time to find another place to spend his time. A safe place where he could find food and water. A place where the smell wasn't as bad.

He had nothing to carry. He had no clothes, books or toys. He stood in front of his home one last time and cried as he thought about leaving his mama, papa, brothers and sisters. He looked to his left and then to his right. He turned to his left again and began walking. He was without a family and home. All he had was a precarious and unknown future.

Chapter 23

Rose

    The car stopped at the edge of the village. James, Marie Lucie and Rose emerged into a shaded yard. The house was small, much smaller than Farah's, but much larger than her papa's on the beach.

    A man appeared in the front door of the painted concrete block house. Immediately Rose assessed what her work load might be at this place. It, being a smaller home, would mean less rooms and less sweeping. If Wilson lived by himself, it would mean less washing, less water to carry and less cooking. There wouldn't be kids to deliver to school. Rose was starting to feel optimistic.

    Her thoughts were interrupted, "Rose, come here and meet Wilson."

    Rose quickly joined the trio and hung her head.

    Wilson held out his hand and said, "Rose, it's good to meet you."

    Rose shook his hand. A quick glance revealed a smile and kind face. Unfortunately, Rose had learned smiles can cover evil intentions. She'd been down that rocky path before. Trust wasn't coming easy these days.

    James said, "Rose, you know what's expected of you. We don't ever want to hear anything bad about you and your work, or how you treat Wilson."

    James and Marie Lucie abruptly got in the car and left. Rose was left standing in a new place with a stranger.

    Making conversation, Wilson casually said, "I lost my wife and two children in the earthquake several years ago when we lived in Port au Prince. I live here alone and I need help in taking care of my place. I'm a busy man with a job and I don't have time for cooking, cleaning and washing."

He turned around and headed to the house. Rose assumed she was to follow.

The house had three rooms and was clean and orderly. There was a bedroom, a kitchen and a room with a couch and chair. The tin-enclosed back porch had a small bed. There was an outdoor kitchen and also a concrete front porch. Rose looked around the clean yard for a hut where she'd be staying. She saw none and for a fleeting and optimistic moment wondered who the back porch bed was for.

After showing Rose the house, they ended up on the concrete front porch. Wilson sat down on a green wooden chair and pointed to the red chair and said, "Rose, you can sit down."

She slid into the chair and waited.

Wilson said, "Tell me about your family."

Rose hesitated.

Wilson looked at her downcast face and saw a scared little girl. Again he said, "Rose, it's okay. Tell me about your family."

Rose began with a brief description of her papa, her sisters and her brother.

She stopped.

Wilson encouraged her, "Go on."

She continued with the story of how her mom had died and how papa hadn't been able to keep his family together and healthy.

Wilson nodded. He seemed to understand.

"Tell me what your village and lakou was like."

"Oh, it was beside the sea. Our home was almost on the beach. Do you know where that is?"

Wilson laughed. "No, I don't know where your home would be. Haiti has 1,100 miles of shoreline and beaches. It could have been almost anywhere."

Rose uncomfortably said, "Isn't there something I need to be doing for you?"

"No, it's good to have someone to talk to. I already have our evening meal ready and the house is clean. Tomorrow you can begin your work."

He continued, "Oh, I didn't see that you brought anything. Where are your clothes and things?"

Rose hesitated and said, "I don't have anything. The last lady I worked for took my things and sold them in the market."

"Oh. Well, I imagine that's another story for another time. We'll have to get you some clothes. The clothes you're wearing are pretty ragged and just might fall off. We can't have you walking around without any clothing!"

Rose laughed with Wilson.

They went into the house and entered the kitchen. There was no refrigerator and it didn't look like Wilson had a generator for electricity.

Wilson retrieved the food from under overturned plastic bowls on the counter. Wilson prayed aloud that God would bless the food. Then he asked God to take care of Rose and to bless her. They ate together at the table.

Rose was feeling hopeful and blessed already.

After cleaning up their meal and washing the pots, pans and dishes, Rose looked around the house. There was a photo of Wilson, a woman and two children. A boy and a girl.

She saw a book on a small table which she had learned from Jesulah was called a Bible. But the most important discovery was nowhere in the house did she see a rigoise! Ah, maybe she had died and entered heaven! Rose laughed to herself until she remembered the open sores on her back.

Wilson took her to the back porch. The small bed with a real mattress and pillow was going to be hers.

Chapter 24

Jean Pierre

He had walked all day. In the afternoon, Jean Pierre joined a group of children shuffling down the road. Multiple times he stopped and peered into the dark depths of large cracks in the highway. The cracks were large and deep enough for him to stand in, but there was no way he'd try that. He wondered if anyone had been swallowed into those crevasses during the earthquake. He shuddered as he thought about what it might have been like to be swallowed up by the earth. Then he remembered again the roar of the monster in Port au Prince. He quickly rejoined the group of boys and girls, some older, some younger as they continued walking together through the city.

He again looked around at his bedraggled traveling companions. Some had open sores. All were extremely dirty. A few had no clothing. None carried any belongings. There were no smiles, only empty and sad faces.

One of the girls was carrying a small baby who seemed to be crying more often than being quiet. He guessed the baby was hungry. The girl was probably about his age, six or seven-years-old. She didn't seem to know what to do with the crying and distraught baby. They kept walking.

They shuffled past so many bodies lying on the streets he no longer kept count. He saw bodies which had been there for days as well as bodies that were recent. He guessed some people were still dying from their injuries.

Some of the bodies were naked. He had noticed people taking clothing off some of the corpses and realized the dead didn't need them anymore. He looked down at his own clothing and realized maybe it wasn't a bad idea. Now, he began searching for a boy his size among the bodies strewn alongside the street.

His head and leg still hurt, but at least they no longer were bleeding or seeping. He was going to be alright.

It wasn't long before he noticed a child lying in the gutter. He went to the corpse. The smell everywhere was the same. Horrible. Putrefying. No way to escape the raunchy odor. Jean Pierre reached down and undid the buttons on the red shirt. Carefully he tugged until he got it loose. So far so good. No one was stopping him. He looked up and noticed no one was watching and he knew then that no one cared.

He did the same thing with the boy's shorts. As he maneuvered the shorts off the stiff and rotting body, he realized he wasn't feeling anything for the boy. His emotions were numb. No tears. No grief. No sadness. He was simply thankful to get different clothes. He proudly grabbed the blue shorts and red shirt and joined his new-found friends. The baby was still crying.

Thirty minutes later, they came to a river. All the children ran down the bank to the water. As Jean Pierre arrived, he saw bodies upstream and downstream lying in the water or on the shore. The stench of rotting bodies was everywhere and he knew drinking this water would bring illness and death.

He yelled to the children, "Don't drink the water. It'll make you sick." The children didn't even pause or look at him. They kept drinking.

He went to the water and began washing the clothes he had just claimed. The cleaning helped to remove most of the stink which had clung to the shirt and shorts.

The group climbed back up to the road. There were hundreds of people leaving the city. He didn't know where he was going, but he knew he had to leave the death and memories of Port au Prince.

The aftershocks were still occurring. There were damaged buildings crumbling again and again. Soon there would be nothing left to fall. There were some homes partially standing, but fear forced the people to live on the streets, under trees or in cars. Everyone was afraid of what was coming next. The aftershocks were a constant reminder that this devastating disaster wasn't finished with them yet.

He saw several men and women trying to use tree branches or broken lumber as a crutch. As they hobbled by, he curiously asked one of the men about his injury.

"I was in my home when the earthquake happened. A large chunk of concrete landed on my leg. My leg didn't break, but I was pinned under the heavy concrete and other rubble for eight hours. Finally rescuers got me out. My leg had no blood circulating for those eight hours."

Then he added with no emotion, "I think it's dead. I'm hoping to find a hospital. I think they'll cut if off."

He had said it so matter-of-factly, it was like the man was talking about someone else.

Jean Pierre looked at the mangled leg. There were gashes, cuts and dried blood. But the most horrifying thing was the color of the leg. It was much blacker than the rest of his brown Haitian skin. It did look like something that needed to be removed. Jean Pierre shuddered as he thought of a machete, saw or knife doing its grisly work.

Darkness came. The children clustered together and slept fitfully listening to the dying baby's weakening cries.

~

Five days after the earthquake, the city was far behind them. He had forgotten how peaceful rural Haiti was. Here along the northwest shoreline, the countryside was relatively flat. He stopped on the road and looked around. He could see mountains upon mountains in the distance. His papa had told him the word Ayiti had come from the original Indians who had lived there. It meant 'Land of Mountains' or 'Mountains beyond Mountains.'

The homes close to the road were still showing a lot of damage. There were some bodies, but fewer than in the city. As the small group got farther from the city, they began to see vehicles on the road. Most were heading west as he was. The drivers didn't stop to help anyone, as they seemed intent to get as far away from Port au Prince as quickly as possible.

The baby had died the night before. The young girl caretaker had laid the baby along the side of the road and covered her with a shirt and walked on. As he had watched the baby being laid gently to the ground, he had cried. Now, he was confronted by the harsh reality of their situation. The baby had died for lack of nutrition and fluids. Those older, such as himself, were heading down the same path toward death as the baby girl. It was just taking longer. He knew they desperately needed to get something to eat. Unfortunately, everyone in this part of Haiti was in the same situation.

A day later they began to pass sugar cane fields. They had stopped and pulled down stalks and began chewing on them. The sweet taste helped for a while, but Jean Pierre knew he had to get something more substantial. His 'borrowed' clothes were drooping on his small diminishing body.

While gathering a few pieces of cane, he asked a man where they were. The man said, "This is Leogane. This is the place the earthquake started. This is the center. The damage here was bad, but not as bad as the slopes in Port au Prince where homes tumbled and rolled onto homes further below."

He continued, "The homes here aren't on slopes but on flatter ground. You should see Port au Prince. It's horrible!"

Jean Pierre walked away without telling him what had happened to his own home and family on those Port slopes. Those memories were still too fresh.

His stomach ached and his body was begging for food. He remembered watching a woman outside her hut eating a meal the day before as they passed. She had paused in her meal just long enough to watch the ragged group of children passing by. He knew the group was too large to feed. He wondered if possibly she'd have fed him something if he'd been alone.

Desperation drove him to a tough decision. He decided to leave the safety and comfort of his shabby group to see if he would have success by himself in finding food. Sadly, he told the group goodbye as he left in search of a kind villager.

He found a path which led inland and up. Walking for ten minutes he found a stream of water. Searching for dead bodies nearby and finding none, he drank his fill and kept walking.

Soon he came upon a small hut. Beyond, he could see multiple small homes. These homes didn't have a concrete roof so the earthquake had done little damage, though this area was very near the epicenter of the quake. One good thing about the poor Haitian huts built with palm thatched roofs and walls is they seemed earthquake resistant. This village was relatively intact.

As he walked, he looked for someone friendly and receptive with whom to communicate. He saw a woman outside one of the homes and approached her.

"Madame, I'm sorry to ask, but I'm very hungry. I've come from Port au Prince."

"Oh my! How did you get here?"

"I walked on the big road."

"Where's your family"?

"My mama, papa, brothers and sisters all died in the earthquake."

"Come in and I'll find you something to eat."

Without hesitation, he followed the woman through the wooden door frame into a modest home.

"I don't have much, but I think I can find something for you."

"Here's some bread, plantains and water."

Jean Pierre thanked her and ravenously wolfed down the food. The woman watched with compassion and pity.

"Where have you been these last days since the earthquake?"

"When my mama and sisters died in our house, I waited for two days for my papa and brothers to come home. They didn't, so I decided to begin walking."

Jean Pierre finished eating, wiped his mouth with the back of his hand and stood up. The woman also stood up and went to him. She held out her hands to him and nearly swallowed the small six-year-old boy into her arms.

He looked up at her and saw tears streaming down her kind face. He began to cry. She sat down on a chair and held him quietly while he sobbed. The pent up emotions of the last days spilled out in his tears. The loss of his family, the horrible things he'd seen, the death, the smell, the screams, moans and wails, the loss of the crying baby, it all came out in a rush.

She held him and patted his back. Finally, the tears stopped and he crumpled to the floor.

"Would you like to sleep here tonight?"

Jean Pierre nodded. This was the first peace he'd known in six days.

Chapter 25

Rose

Rose was beginning to understand there were different kinds of restavek families. It seemed Farah was one type and Wilson was another.

Though Rose worked hard for him, she received food, a bed and a home to live in. More importantly to her was the sense of love and care Wilson seemed to have for her. It seemed he still had a hole in his heart from the loss of his wife and children. Somehow Rose sensed she was filling part of that hole.

After living with Wilson for a few days, she knew he was a good man. He read the Bible and often read it to her. She was gradually learning the difference between 'knowing good' and 'doing good.' Wilson seemed to practice what he read in the Bible.

While living with Carlos and Farah, Rose had been obedient out of fear. With Wilson, she was learning obedience out of respect and love. In many ways, living with Wilson reminded her of her own family and home.

One day while they were talking together, Wilson paused and said, "Rose, I want to tell you a story. It's a true story that gives me hope for our country. It's about a restavek girl who lived with a pastor and his wife. He didn't beat her, but he worked her very hard. She didn't go to school or church and certainly wasn't treated like his own children.

"One day the pastor was invited to a seminar about restavek children. The pastors were taught what the Bible says about caring for orphans and vulnerable children. They were challenged to preach to their church congregations and neighbors about how to care for them.

"The pastor went home after two days of listening. He called the restavek girl to him and said, 'Get your things and leave.'

"They walked out the front door of the house together. The pastor said, 'You can no longer live in our house as a restavek.'

"She began walking until the pastor called her back almost immediately and said, 'we took you in as a restavek and we've sent you away as a restavek. Now, I want to invite you back to our home so you can live here as our daughter.' From that day on, she was treated like the other children in his family. She began to go to school and church and the people of the community watched and respected it very much. Others started to do the same to their restavek children. God blesses those who care for orphans and vulnerable children like He commands in the Bible."

Wilson continued, "I don't have much Rose, but I'll do my best to treat you like you deserve and like the Bible says."

Rose hadn't felt this safe and loved since she had left her papa, family and their home.

After hearing the story, Rose summoned up the courage to ask a question. "Thanks for telling me about the pastor and the restavek girl. Hearing that made me very happy. Do you think there would be a way you could send me back to my papa and family?"

"Rose, that's the reason I asked you to tell me about your lakou and village. I thought you might know where you had lived. But it seems all you remember is living by the beach.

Unless you remember something else, there's no way to find your home. I can't ask James and Marie Lucie as they would simply take you away again. I'm not sure there's anything we can do." Then with hesitation, he said, "I'm sorry. I would if I could."

Rose's heart broke. Though Wilson was treating her very well, there wouldn't have been anything better than getting back to her family. Rose was sensing she might never see her family again.

~

On the fifth day at Wilson's home, he took Rose to the village well. When they arrived she couldn't believe what she saw. This was Carice, the same village and pump she had gone to for Farah's family. Now, she was entering the clearing from the other direction. Rose had no idea she was so close to Farah's house. The last thing she wanted was to run into Mad Dog Farah.

Then it hit her, *I wonder if I'll get to see Jesulah again.* She couldn't wait to tell her what had happened. Though she recognized some of the children at the pump she didn't see Jesulah.

Two days later they met at the well.

Jesulah and Rose hugged each another. Anyone watching would have thought they were long lost sisters.

"What happened to you? Suddenly you were gone and I had no idea why you left or if I'd ever see you again. Now, here you are! I can't believe you're here and you're okay!"

Rose told her what had happened at Carlo's and Farah's home on that horrible night. She shared how she came to be living at Wilson's.

Jesulah smiled and said, "I see a smile on your face. I can see this was a good change for you. I didn't think I'd ever see you again."

"Yes, it's been a good thing. It's almost like he's treating me like a daughter. He said I could go to church with him next Sunday! I still can't believe it! Can you imagine, sitting on a bench in church? I won't have to sit outside under the window."

Then she added, "I'm sorry Jesulah. I didn't mean to say I have it better than you."

"I know you didn't. I'm really happy for you. We'll be at the same church at the same time, just a wall apart from each other. That'll be special!"

~

The next day began just like any other day at Wilson's house. He had left after breakfast for his work in the next town. His routine was always leaving after breakfast and returning in the late afternoon. He was a mason and was busy laying blocks at a small hotel and restaurant being built twenty minutes up the road.

A smile came to Rose's face as she realized Wilson seemed to enjoy telling her at supper about his day. He would talk about the people he'd met and how the work was going. He enjoyed having someone listening to him and Rose happily soaked up his words.

Finishing her chores, she began fixing soup, plantains and fruit for their evening meal.

She waited for Wilson's small car to rattle into the lakou.

Then the sun began to set.

She continued to wait.

It became dark. She worried. She ate her meal. Now, the worry was turning into a growing sense of fear.

She went to bed and slept fitfully.

A rooster crowed and Rose opened her eyes to another dawn in Haiti.

Going to his bedroom, Rose expected to see Wilson sleeping.

He wasn't there and the bed was still unslept in.

She fixed herself a small breakfast and began her chores.

At noon, she heard a car coming closer. Expectantly she stood on the front porch and waited. It wasn't Wilson. Rather, it was a car she'd not seen before. A man, not Wilson, emerged.

He walked to the house and said, "Who are you?"

"I'm Rose."

"What are you doing here?"

"I stay with Wilson, cleaning his house and fixing his meals."

The man sat wearily on the front porch chair and told Rose to have a seat.

He said, "My name is Claudin. Wilson and I are friends and work together as masons. Yesterday, Wilson didn't come to work which was very unusual. He's usually the first to arrive. We began our work and he never showed up. After work yesterday I decided to come here and see if he was sick. On the way, I saw his car demolished beside the road. A large truck had lost control and crashed into him on a curve when he was coming to work yesterday."

Pausing, he then continued, "Wilson was killed in the accident. I'm so sorry to tell you about it."

Rose didn't know what to say. She began crying. She had grown to respect and appreciate Wilson. Now she was feeling incredibly sad and scared. Another loss. More grief. More fear. She had thought her life was going in a good direction. What now?

Her list of questions about life was getting longer, not shorter.

Through her tears, she thought she heard the man talking. She said, "I'm sorry, what did you say?"

"I asked you what you were going to do and where you were going to go?"

"Uh... I don't know. I don't know where my family is. I don't have anywhere to go. I only know how to work."

"Where were you before coming to live with Wilson? Maybe I can take you there?"

"No! I can't go back there!"

"Do you want me to find another place for you?"

Rose waited a minute, pondering the many questions and finally said, "I guess so."

"You stay here tonight as usual. I'll ask around and see if anyone has work for you. I'll be back tomorrow afternoon."

With that, he got in his car and left an incredibly sad, scared, helpless and hopeless Rose alone.

~

The next morning Rose took care of her chores. Feeling very sad, she grabbed her empty bucket and headed to the well. The day before, Jesulah and Rose had coordinated their timing so they'd arrive at the same time.

Rose's eyes teared up as she said, "I just found out Wilson was killed in a car accident."

"Oh no! You were so happy at his home and he was so nice to you."

"I know. I can't believe it. Just as my life was beginning to get better, this happens."

"What are you going to do? Where are you going to go?"

"I don't know. A friend of his is stopping by this afternoon about some new work for me. I guess I'm just waiting."

"When will you leave?"

"I don't know. I'll find out later today. I just know I can't stay in his house much longer. It's not mine. Someone will take it over."

Rose continued, "Jesulah, I'm not sure I'll ever see you again, but I wanted you to know how much you've meant to me. You've been the only happiness I've had while I was at Farah's and now. I thank God in my prayers for giving you to me as a friend."

"That's really nice of you to say that, but you know I feel the same way about you."

They got their water in silence.

Hugging Jesulah, Rose said, "Keep eavesdropping at church. I think both of us have learned a lot from that. Maybe someday I'll see you again. It looks like my dream of being in church on Sunday isn't going to happen."

A few tears, another hug and then both headed in opposite directions.

Chapter 26

Jean Pierre

Jean Pierre woke the next morning and couldn't believe his luck. He had gotten something to eat from a kind woman and a place to sleep. Then, he remembered the earthquake and the life he had prior to it. He'd had many good nights of sleep when he had been with his family.

He felt ashamed that he hadn't been thinking much about his family the last few days.

He heard noises from another part of the house. Getting out of bed, he walked toward the noise and found the woman eating at a small table.

"Ah, the slumbering child awakens!"

Jean Pierre smiled. She reminded him of his mother.

"Come and join me for some bread."

He tried to eat slowly and politely, but he was still really hungry. She pretended not to notice and put more bread in front of him.

"I'm sorry I don't have more to eat. It's been difficult these last days. Many people are very afraid they'll run out of food. I can't imagine what life is like in Port au Prince. Here at least we can grow our own fruit and vegetables."

Jean Pierre said, "There were many hungry people in Port after the earthquake. I don't know what they'll do. I didn't see anyone helping anybody."

"Oh, I'm sure people will come to help, but it'll take a while. I'm sorry, I didn't even ask your name?"

"My name is Jean Pierre."

"Well, Jean Pierre, I think we'll need to find out what to do with you. Oh, my name is Luise."

~

Later that afternoon, Jean Pierre stretched out in Madame Luise's yard under a breadfruit tree. He tried to count the breadfruit overhead and hoped none of them would fall on him. Some of the rough skinned green fruit were the size of coconuts.

Madame Luise had left the lakou earlier and was just returning.

Jean Pierre got up, dusted himself off and waited for her.

"Come into the house, Jean Pierre. Let's talk."

Entering the house, they sat at her table. Luise said, "A friend of mine lives in a village close by. I know they were looking for a helper in their home before the earthquake. I think they'd treat you kindly. It would be hard work, but you'd have a place to stay and enough to eat. Would you like to do that?"

"I guess I don't have anywhere else to go except back on the road. I think this would be better."

"Okay, let's go meet the family."

~

After a fifteen minute walk farther inland, they arrived in a small village. Madame Luise walked directly to a small house surrounded by mango, coconut and breadfruit trees, along with banana and false banana plants.

Jean Pierre liked the atmosphere of the lakou. All the greenery made it seem like a thriving and warm place. The earthquake seemed a million miles away. As they approached, a short stocky man and similarly shaped woman emerged from the home to greet Madame Luise.

Jean Pierre shuffled his feet and looked at the ground. He wasn't sure what he should be doing, so he waited. The woman came to him and said, "Jean Pierre, my name is Fabienne. My husband is Ronald."

He looked up and saw a wide smile and warm eyes. Ronald stuck a large hand in front of him, so he shook it. He felt a hand full of strength with rough skin.

"Welcome to our home Jean Pierre," he said.

Ronald continued, "Let me show you around and then you can decide if you want to stay with us."

Ronald walked him toward the trees while Fabienne escorted Luise into their home.

"I make a living for us with our trees. We have quite a number and it takes work to collect and sell the coconuts, mangoes, bananas, breadfruit and oranges."

Jean Pierre enjoyed eating anything that came from a Haitian tree, so this was sounding like a pretty nice oasis.

They went into the house where Fabienne showed him the rooms. In one of the rooms, Fabienne said, "This is where you would sleep."

Ronald said, "We need help with our work. You're only six-years-old and not very big, but I like the idea of training a boy when he's young, rather than older. I'll bet you can climb a coconut tree like a monkey. What do you think? Would you like to live here?"

Jean Pierre looked at Ronald, then at Fabienne. He turned to look at Luise who was nodding her head 'yes.'

He said, "Yes."

Chapter 27

Rose

Claudin came walking up the path to the door of Wilson's house. Rose stopped mopping the front concrete porch and watched him approach. She had been concerned all day that he wouldn't come as he had promised.

"Hello Rose. We should talk."

Seated on the porch in the red and green chairs, Claudin said to Rose, "I think I've found a home for you. Gather the things you have and we'll go meet someone."

Rose collected the few things which Wilson had given her, placed them in a plastic bag and followed Claudin to the car.

When they got to the car, Rose asked Claudin, "Do you think it would be okay for me to take Wilson's Bible?"

"He won't be needing it. Go ahead."

Quickly, Rose ran to the house, grabbed the Bible and ran back to the car. She couldn't read, but just holding the Bible brought a warm feeling to her heart.

Following roads which looked more like trails, in ten minutes they arrived in front of a small, very poor looking home. It reminded her of her papa's hut. This one however, did have concrete walls instead of thatch. There was rusty tin on the roof and the door was unpainted as were the shutters. The major difference between this lakou and her papa's was the yard full of rubbish. Claudin got out and said, "Stay in the car until I talk to Jude."

A tall, thin, bald man came out of the home and Rose assumed it was Jude. He and Claudin talked for several minutes.

Claudin came to the car and said, "Rose, you'll be staying with this man. His name is Jude."

Rose sat quietly, contemplating her future.

Claudin said, "Come out of the car Rose!"

She obeyed.

The car started and Claudin drove away. He seemed anxious to leave.

She rooted herself to the path, looking down. Forty feet away was the home and the waiting Jude.

Jude said, "Rose, come here."

Rose obeyed quickly and stood in front of him.

He rudely turned around and went into the house. She followed.

There were only two small rooms in the home. One room served as a living area which included a small bed and a chair. Looking through the doorway she saw a small table with a single chair in what served as a kitchen.

Rose was glad to see concrete floors in the home. That would make it easier to keep them clean. You can mop concrete, but you can't mop dirt. When it rained, dirt in a hut usually turned into a sticky mess due to leaking roofs. She looked up and noticed the roof was in decent shape. Another blessing.

Jude looked at her and said, "I live here by myself and need help with the work around the home. I know you've lost your place to live so I can let you live here if you work for me. It'll be better than if you were on your own or living in the streets of Port au Prince."

Jude continued to look at her, waiting for a response and finally said, "Are you able to talk?"

Rose reluctantly replied, "Yes."

"Well, then say something!"

Stammering, she said, "Thank you for giving me a place to stay."

"You can stay here as long as you do what I say. I can't have you here if you disobey me or cause any problems. If that would happen, I'll punish you, and believe me, that won't be a good thing."

"Do you have any questions?"

With hesitation, Rose asked, "Will I be able to go to school or church?"

Laughing, Jude said, "No, you won't have time for any of that stuff."

"Any other questions?"

With her head hanging, Rose wagged her head with a mute 'no.'

~

As dusk approached, Jude took her to the room with the table and chair.

Pointing under the table, he said, "This is where you'll sleep. I've got a blanket you can use."

Taking her to the back door, he pointed to the steps and said, "This is where you'll eat."

She followed him down the three cluttered concrete steps as he walked to the outdoor cooking area. "This is where you'll prepare my food."

Everything, beginning at the front of the house, under the table, on the back steps, the back yard including the cooking area was cluttered with rags, cans, paper and litter. It seemed

Jude had been waiting a long time for someone like Rose to clean up his chaotic mess.

He said, "I already had my food for tonight and there's nothing left for you. Tomorrow you can begin by making my breakfast. You'll be able to eat then. You can go to bed now, but be sure to be out of bed when the sun begins to rise."

He brought her a blanket. Rose cringed as she looked at the dried mud and dirt clinging to it. Unfortunately there was a nasty smell hanging on to it just as tightly as the dirt. She knew cleaning the blanket in the morning would be a must. She threw it aside.

She cleared the floor under the table and crawled into her 'bed.' Once again it seemed she was dealing with the mountains and valleys of Haiti. Farah had been a really deep valley that Rose never wanted to visit again. Wilson had been a mountain-top experience and it appeared only time would tell what kind of a master Jude would be.

Though she didn't like the cramped space under the table, at least it wasn't corrugated tin she was trying to get comfortable on. On another note, she hadn't yet seen a rigoise anywhere around the house and that made her smile. There was the good and there was the bad.

Chapter 28

Jean Pierre

Just a week after the earthquake, Jean Pierre found himself living with Ronald and Fabienne. As the days and months rolled on, he found the work to be long and hard, but they fed him regularly and treated him kindly. Ronald had recognized Jean Pierre was young, small and had no experience in taking care of trees, but was patient in teaching him every day.

~

The years went by. Jean Pierre just had his thirteenth birthday and was surprised when Ronald and Fabienne had a small surprise celebration party for him. After the few guests had left, the three of them sat and talked.

Ronald said, "Jean Pierre, you've been a valuable help to Fabienne and me. There's no way we could've managed as well as we have without you. Last night, she and I talked about how small and young you were when you came here. You've learned a lot since then and you're a strong young man now."

He continued, "I know we haven't paid you for your years of work. There was no way we could, but we hope that giving you a home, food and clothing has meant something to you."

Jean Pierre said, "When I came, I had lost everything. I remember walking on the road with the other children trying to get away from Port au Prince. I can still remember the things I saw from the earthquake. The crushed buildings, the dead people, the smells and the sounds. That was a really bad time.

I remember how happy I was to find a place to live. You've treated me kindly and I'm happy here. I also know I'm learning things that will help me as I get older."

"Yes, you've learned well and you know how to care for all the different kinds of trees we have. You know about their cycles and how to help them produce even more fruit. You know all about selling the products. We've trusted you with our money and we've never been disappointed. We hope you want to stay with us. We've never had children of our own and you're like a son to us."

Fabienne gave him a hug. She hadn't done that for a long time and it felt good.

Jean Pierre said, "I know I'm a restavek, but I also know I have it much better than many other restaveks I know. My life could have been very different."

He continued, "Just yesterday I met a new restavek at the market who lives with Jude. None of the kids I know have anything good to say about him. I think the girl's problems are only beginning. I think she's eleven-years-old. Her name is Rose."

Fabienne said, "Yes, we know Jude. He doesn't have a very good reputation even though he's the voodoo houngan. No one will ever say anything bad about him to his face, but people talk. People are afraid of what he could do."

Jean Pierre said, "I really feel bad for Rose. She's already been through a lot. She had been with Carlos and Farah, then Wilson and now with Jude. That's a lot of moving around. She doesn't look happy or healthy and she's really thin."

Ronald said, "Ah, yes, I remember. Wilson was killed in that car accident up the road last week. That was a sad thing that happened to a good man. I wondered what would happen to the girl living with him."

Fabienne said, "I knew Carlos and Farah recently got a new girl. I wondered what had happened to the girl they had who you call Rose. It was really sad what happened to the girl before her. She became really sick and then died. It seems Carlos and Farah run through restaveks like flour through a sieve."

Jean Pierre said, "Well, I feel really bad for Rose, so when I see girls or boys like her, I know I'm really fortunate."

Chapter 29

Rose

Rose was learning more and more about Jude. Overall, he didn't seem to be a bad person, he just had some major issues. Rose realized that her idea of who was good and who was bad was changing. Instead of measuring others based on what she knew of her mama and papa, she found herself comparing people to Farah.

First of all, Jude simply didn't take time to care for himself, his home or his things. Now that he had a restavek helper, he expected a clean, tidy house and yard. Rose spent several days getting the garbage and trash cleaned up to a level where he was satisfied.

She also learned he was probably thin for reasons other than genetics. There simply wasn't enough food for him or Rose. She noticed her ribs were becoming more pronounced.

Jude also loved his alcohol. Fortunately for Rose, when he drank too much, he feel asleep rather than becoming rude or angry. She'd seen plenty of rudeness and anger in other men in the last few years. She'd been taken advantage of more often than she wanted to remember.

When she had first arrived at Jude's home, Rose was intrigued by an outdoor shelter in the courtyard, covered by tin and open on the sides. In the middle of the shelter was a knee-high, round, concrete pedestal. Rising from the pedestal to the roof was a round pole painted red and blue. Halfway up the pole, a broom was attached by a rope. At the edge of the shelter was a three foot wooden cross embedded in concrete. Surrounding the cross were bottles of alcohol, a cola bottle and a few more. Above the tin roof were four flags of various colors flying in the breeze. Rose had wondered what it all meant.

She didn't have long to wait.

The next day, on a Saturday morning, Jude said, "I have a group coming tonight for a ceremony and I need you there."

"What kind of ceremony?"

"I'm a houngan priest and we're going to have a voodoo ceremony. I want you to watch and learn."

Later that afternoon, people began arriving. Bottles of alcohol were opened and the group became louder. A set of drums began hammering out African rhythms which undoubtedly had been brought to the island hundreds of years earlier by African slaves.

After dark, the many lit candles were creating dancing shadows in the open courtyard. Rose shuddered. The shadows didn't seem to be from the dancing people, or were they? She wondered what was happening.

Soon Jude and others were drunkenly, yet skillfully dancing around the pole. The dancing went on and on until Jude fell to the ground writhing and shaking. Though Rose had no idea what was happening, it was apparent the group was focused in their intentions and purpose.

Later that night at home, Jude said, "Rose, I hope you were watching what happened tonight. I want you to dance in the future when we do the ceremonies. The dancing is something that encourages the loa spirits to visit us. I think they would like a young girl like you dancing."

Rose asked, "What are the loa spirits?"

"God is too distant from us. We need intermediaries. We use our ceremonies to bring the invisible loa spirits to us. When the spirits arrive, they tell me things which can be used to help others. They are the spirits or souls of the dead."

Rose remembered how Jude had suddenly been thrown to the ground and she shuddered as she thought of the dark, shadowy and mysterious world of voodoo. She trembled as she realized Jude's expectations of her involvement.

Again he said, "I'll need you to dance for the spirits whenever we have our ceremonies."

~

As the weeks and months continued, Rose was becoming more and more hopeless of things changing. There were days she felt ill. She had chills and a fever at times, but there was no mercy from Jude to relax from her work. She simply and obediently kept working.

She knew if she didn't find more food, she'd eventually starve to death. Occasionally she would get handouts from an elderly woman in the village named Joanna.

Once when Rose passed by Joanna's hut, she said, "Rose, I wish I could have you come to my home and live with me. I could use your help. But I know Jude would never let you leave him. He has powers that can be used for good or evil. I've known him for many years and I don't want to cross him, but once in a while I can give you a little to eat. I don't have much, but I'll help you when I can."

The bread and plantains Joanna supplied weren't enough to satisfy the gnawing hunger growing in Rose's stomach. She knew she wasn't alone as nearly all restaveks seemed thin and hungry.

One afternoon while at the river bathing, Rose saw something she'd never seen before. Two children were sitting on the river bank and digging in the dirt. Then she saw them put the dirt in their mouth.

Walking over to them, she said, "Why are you eating dirt?"

The older one said, "It's the only way we can stop the hunger pains."

"Well, that can't be good for you."

With a smirk, he said, "I suppose being hungry all the time is a good thing?"

Rose watched as they continued to eat the dirt.

Walking away, she cried for the children. She felt the same hunger the children did, but couldn't believe things could get so bad someone could eat dirt.

Rose knew about stomach pain. She knew there were worms in her stomach which she was sharing her food with. When she went to the toilet, sometimes she'd see them. It made her shudder to know something was living inside her.

A few weeks later she again saw something she hadn't seen before. An elderly woman in the open market was buying a flat piece of food that looked like a round thick cracker. Watching from a few feet away she saw the woman pass a single gourde coin to the seller.

The woman walked away eating the cracker. Rose approached the market lady and asked, "What did that woman buy from you?"

"Oh, it was a cookie."

"It only cost one gourde?"

"Yes, do you want one?"

"I don't have a gourde."

Waving her hand as if she were chasing away a fly, the seller said, "Then don't bother me."

Rose left, but kept her eyes on the ground looking for a stray gourde.

Several days later at the well, Rose found a five gourde coin in the dirt. She knew immediately what she was going to do with it!

The next day she went to the market to get food for Jude. She found the lady with the cookies and bought one. Excited to have a cookie in her hand and an extra four gourde coins in her pocket, she retreated to a shady tree at the edge of the market.

The cookie had a smooth yellowish-tan surface. It was hard and had creamy swirls on top. She took a small bite and found it was hard and brittle. A piece broke off in her mouth. She chewed it and found it tasted like dirt! She spit it on the ground.

She went back to the market lady and asked, "Is this dirt?"

"Yes, of course. What did you think you were buying?"

"What's in it?"

"Some salt, shortening, dirt and water. They're dried in the sun. Some people say they're really healthy and full of nutrients, especially for pregnant women. Some people call them mud cookies."

Rose went back to the tree and continued nibbling. Once the dirt was in her mouth it soaked up her saliva and became very difficult to swallow. She headed to the river and drank water while eating it. Now she knew why the children were eating dirt by the river.

She was now officially a dirt-eater and didn't like how that sounded.

~

Rose woke with a chill and knew she had another fever. She wondered if the dirt she had eaten was creating problems. She also knew she'd have to work today, just like she had been working every day for the last year for Jude.

Crawling out from under the table, she began her day. Grabbing her buckets, she headed to the village well where she saw Jean Pierre getting water for Ronald and Fabienne. She was always happy to see him. Though he was a restavek, she knew his situation was probably the best of the best. He lived with a family who cared about him, fed him and gave him a potentially good future. Not very many restaveks were that fortunate.

"Hi Rose. Are you doing okay?"

Rose never knew how to answer that question. She thought to herself... *I don't get enough to eat; I have no family; no one is looking out for me; I can't go to church or school; I sleep under a table; I work from dawn to dusk; I get beaten; no one cares about a restavek; I'm treated worse than a dog or goat; I get fevers; my stomach hurts almost all the time; I eat dirt. How am I doing?*

She said, "I'm doing okay."

Jean Pierre smiled and said, "That's good to hear. It's always good to see you."

Realistically, he knew she wasn't telling the truth. Rose was not doing 'okay.'

She smiled and waited her turn at the pump.

Returning home, Jude gave her 250 gourdes and said, "Rose! I need beer from the market. Go buy me six bottles and make sure they're cold. Bring the extra coins back to me. Hurry!"

Rose headed out the door and walked quickly to the market. She knew Jude's patience level got shorter and shorter without his precious alcohol. Months ago, she had taken her time on the way back with his beer and regretted that. She found out then that there was a rigoise in the house.

The man in the market took the six bottles out of an old refrigerator that no longer worked. Ice chunks were stored in the refrigerator which kept the drinks cold.

He quickly placed the six brown bottles in a plastic bag. Rose grabbed the bag and headed down the small road leading to her path which would take her back to Jude's home.

Hurrying down the road, she heard a sharp clunk, then a clatter. Looking down she saw the six bottles of beer lying on the dusty road. Peering into her sack she saw the bottom had torn under the weight.

It almost seemed funny to her as she remembered an old saying her papa had told her. *'An empty sack can't stand up.'*

As quickly as she thought it was funny, a heavy feeling settled over her as she wondered if any bottles had broken. She knew there'd be a price to pay for that mistake!

She was relieved to see none of the bottles had broken.

The hole in the bottom of the sack was too large to hold any of the bottles. She threw the sack down and decided to try and carry the bottles back in her hands. She picked up two of the bottles and added the third. Then with three captured between her small fingers, she tried to add a fourth. Soon all four were on the ground again. She tried again and again to no avail. She looked in disbelief at this tragedy unfolding before her eyes. She knew Jude would be incredibly angry if she had to make two trips or if she broke even one bottle.

The chills, fever, overload of work, fear of the rigoise and watching six bottles of beer beginning to warm on the dusty road, overcame her with waves of fear and terror. Her heart raced as she began panting for another breath. Then she did what came naturally. She collapsed on the dusty rutted road and burst into tears. Soon, she was sobbing uncontrollably.

Rose desperately wanted to run away at that moment. She knew there was the despised rigoise waiting for her if she didn't get home soon. But her desire to run was always stymied by the question, *'Where would I go?'* and *'What will they do to my family?'*

Weeping in the road, two shoes appeared next to the beer. Looking up, she saw a white man looking down at her. He said something in a language she didn't understand. He knelt down beside her and said something again. He put his hand on her shoulder and Rose recoiled as if she'd been stung. He pulled back his hand, said something again and smiled at her.

Still crying, she pointed to the ripped plastic bag. He looked at her and the six bottles of beer. A sudden understanding lit his eyes. Kneeling down beside her, he picked up the bag, tied two small knots in the bottom and nestled the six bottles into the repaired sack. He held the full bag up to her, placing one of her hands under the bag and the other grasping the top.

He began talking, again in an unknown language. He was still holding her hands with the bag as he spoke. She looked in his eyes and saw kindness and compassion. She couldn't believe it. This man had tears running down his face. As he talked, she recognized only one word... 'Jesus.'

She stopped crying, realizing she'd just been rescued from a horrible rigoise beating. With a tear streaked face, she smiled at the kind man and quietly said, "Mesi anpil, mesi anpil, mesi anpil," hoping he'd understand her thankfulness. He smiled and she realized he did understand. She hurriedly walked down the road. Turning around she saw the man still standing there. She was confused.

Arriving at Jude's house, she gave him the beer and the remaining gourdes. He said nothing as he opened a bottle. She quickly disappeared from his sight and continued her work.

She wondered about the man who had helped her on the road. *Why would a stranger help me? Especially, why would a white man go out of his way to assist a restavek? Why did he shed tears for me? What did he want in return? Why did a stranger have to be the one helping? Why didn't a Haitian man help? What was wrong with this culture?*

Then she remembered something Jesulah had heard from the pastor as she eavesdropped at the church. "Jesus said we should love our neighbors as much as we love ourselves. If we do that, things will go well for us."

Then Rose remembered the one word the man on the road had said. 'Jesus.' She believed she understood what it meant to put Jesus's words into action.

Her heart was touched. She cried.

Later that day, Rose stopped by the hut of the elderly Joanna. She told her the story about the beer, plastic bag and the white man.

Then she asked, "Joanna, why did the white man cry when he saw my problem?"

"I don't think he was crying about your beer and sack problem, he was crying because he saw an eleven-year-old restavek girl in trouble. He was crying for you."

"I'd never met him before. Why would he care about me, a stranger?"

"No one knows for sure what's in a person's heart and mind, especially in a white man's mind. My parents and grandparents told me many things about our past. I can think of a few reasons why he may have helped. All of us as Haitians descended from African people who were brought here as slaves by the Spaniards and French. The African slaves began several revolutions against the white men over 200 years ago. The 500,000 slaves finally overthrew the white slavers and became free. Even though they were free, they had no money, education or experience as to how to begin their own country and government. So, other countries and men from abroad continued to exploit them."

She continued, "There are now white people who feel very badly about how the African slaves were treated. They seem anxious to help. Maybe guilt is the reason he helped.

"Africans had been slaves for hundreds of years on the island. They were treated horribly. They didn't get an education, couldn't go to church, rarely got enough to eat, were beaten with rigoise for almost any reason, and forced to work from dawn to dusk. Their sons and daughters were abused and tormented. Their lives were horrible."

Rose interrupted, "I didn't know that. It sounds like the African slaves back then were treated the same as restaveks are treated today."

Joanna said, "Yes, you're right. It's no different. Except now it isn't white men enslaving Haitians. It's Haitians enslaving Haitians."

Rose said, "If Jude, Farah and other Haitians descended from the African slaves, why would they continue to have their own slaves? I don't understand. You'd think they'd want something different than slavery in their own country today. Why would Haitians have Haitian slaves?"

"Yes, you'd think Haitians would want something different than what happened to their families in the past. But the restavek culture has been going on for many, many years. It doesn't change quickly or easily. Many Haitians live in poverty. Some feel they deserve something better so they take in a restavek to do their work. Maybe they believe the restavek has it better being a slave than being alone on the streets without food. Who knows? Maybe the white man knows the Haitian culture won't change easily so he did something small to help at least one restavek."

"Well, I don't know the reason he helped, but I do know he saved me from a terrible rigoise beating. I'm thankful he cared."

Joanna said, "I don't like what happens to restaveks either. But, we shouldn't forget some restaveks are treated very well. You've told me about Jean Pierre who lives with Ronald and Fabienne. That has been a really good thing for him!

"But, it's very hard to go against our culture. Some people make excuses for how they treat a restavek. People feel justified in keeping them. Some say they are following the Bible's teaching by taking a child off the streets. They don't talk about how they abuse the girl or boy, but we know it happens. Not all Haitians keep restaveks. Some take an orphan in as their own child. I've seen it and it's a beautiful thing. I think that's what God wants. But, He's against slavery, no matter how we dress it up.

"I think Rose, someday, God will raise up a Haitian man or woman who will lead this country to stand against restavek abuse."

Chapter 30

Evens

It was dark. Everything around Osnel smelled of earth. A sliver of light came from directly overhead. His bare feet were wet because he was standing in mud.

With a short handled shovel in his hands, he scooped mud from around his feet into a bucket by his side. He paused. He looked up and pulled as much air into his lungs as he could.

Another shovel full. The plastic bucket was getting fuller as he continued digging the four foot diameter hand-dug well in the tight quarters.

He tugged on the rope and immediately his helpers above pulled the full bucket up and lowered an empty.

At the beginning, he had dug through two feet of really hard compacted soil. Then the digging went much easier for the next couple of days. When he hit gravel at twenty feet, he thought water would be coming in soon, but then he hit more rocks and then more dirt. He kept digging. Now there was a bit of water coming into the hole creating the assumption that soon he'd be finished. He was excited to get another well almost completed.

He had started digging wells fifteen years ago. It took experience and a lot of courage to be this deep in the earth. He knew it was a dangerous job and it wasn't for everyone. Though he often thought about finding easier work, he had a reputation as a well-digger and it seemed he never ran out of work. With a wife and five children at home there was a need to bring home the Haitian gourdes.

Nothing made him happier than finishing a well and seeing a village explode with joy upon receiving a steady supply of clean water. Generally he'd emerge from the well to see a crowd of yelling and clapping villagers. That was exciting!

Sometimes his work meant digging a new well, but often the old wells no longer produced water and he needed to dig them another five or ten feet deeper. So, his work continued.

He wondered if he should someday introduce his oldest son, seven-year-old Evens, to this work. It would likely be a steady job for him, but he really wanted him to finish school and get a risk-free job that didn't require muscles and courage.

Soon, the two men on top who were emptying his buckets and handling the bucket-ropes would pull him out of this hole. Osnel smiled as he realized how much he needed to keep his rope-puller men paid well. A well-digger didn't need assistants who didn't like their boss.

His rambling thoughts suddenly stopped as he was hit by a small rock, then a smattering of dirt. He quickly looked up to see the sunlight disappear as his workplace imploded. His life ended in darkness.

~

Evens walked up the path to his home. His mama and little sister were usually in the yard when he returned from school, but he didn't see them. Entering the home, he saw Mama sitting on a kitchen chair crying. His aunt was standing by her side patting her on the back.

"What's the matter Mama?"

His aunt looked at him with tear-filled eyes and said, "Your mama is crying because there was an accident today. As your papa was digging the well, the dirt fell in and he was buried."

With wide eyes he looked from his aunt to his mama and back to his aunt. She simply and numbly nodded her head. Evens went to his mama and put his head on her lap and cried.

He remembered the many times he had gone to the different wells over the last couple of years to see his dad at work. Sometimes he'd holler down the shaft, "Papa... Papa...!"

Then the reply would eerily come up and out of the hole with an echo, "Hello from the center of the earth!" The men above and Evens would laugh. He admired his papa's courage for going into the earth-holes again and again.

~

After the funeral, Mama said to Evens, "Without your papa's gourdes, you won't be able to continue school. I know how much you enjoy it and I also know you're very bright. I'm so sorry."

"Without Papa's money, what can we do to buy food and clothes?"

"It's going to be hard. You might have to work to bring money to our family."

~

Four months later, a neighbor stopped by the hut and asked Evens mother, "How are things with your family?"

"It's been really tough. When my husband was alive, we were able to get by. Now, it's getting harder. I've had to take two children out of school and we aren't getting enough to eat. I'm afraid for my family."

The neighbor looked at each of the five children in the yard. She could see their clothing was tattered and the children were getting thinner. She noticed the older children weren't smiling and seemed quiet.

"I can see it's hard for you. With your four children and the baby, I'm sure it's difficult to support your family without market sales or work. How old is your baby?"

"He's seven-months-old. My husband loved him and all our children very much."

"I know someone who lost a baby son a few months ago. I'm sure they would be very happy to raise your baby. If you'd like me to ask them, I could?"

"No! There's no way I could do that!"

"But, how will you cope with five children?"

"The baby's small. Letting him go wouldn't change anything. He's still nursing. He doesn't take away food from the rest."

"Yes, but he will soon."

With desperation, Mama said, "What I really need is a way to bring money into our home, now."

"Well, that'd be the answer for almost every family in Haiti. You know that seventy percent of Haitians have no jobs, don't you? How could you get a job?"

"I can't, but my oldest son could. He's young and eager to help. He might only be seven, but he's a good worker."

"Do you want me to find someone who needs a helper? Someone who would provide some gourdes for your family?"

"I need to talk to Evens about it first. I'll need some time to think about it too."

~

Two weeks later Evens became a restavek. His mama came to understand she'd have to do something drastic or her family would never return from the slippery slope of poverty. She knew what lay at the bottom of that slope. She hoped Evens could bring home a few gourdes for their family. But she also knew the risk of a child going to another family as restavek and possibly never hearing from them again. Seeing her son leave home created yet more grief and loss for her and her family.

~

Evens began to work for a farmer who lived ten miles from his mama's home. He lived with their family and his life daily grew more difficult. The work inside the home as well as in the hot fields was never-ending. The family raised tobacco, corn and Congo beans which meant year-around work.

The farmer had a wooden depot where he stored his seeds and his harvest. It also became Evens home. It was at least dry and gave him shelter.

After a hard day in the fields and yet more work in the house, he would sit outside the depot and listen to the farmers family. He became envious and angry as he heard them laughing, playing games and eating their meals together. He was hungry, not only for food, but for affirmation, attention, family and love.

Though the farmer had said he would pay Evens for his work, there were no gourdes going into his pocket. He had nothing to send to his family.

As the months wore on, the work increased. It seemed to start earlier and end later. Five days a week he watched the farmer's children leaving for school and coming home. He watched as they played in the lakou. The lights at night in the home were supplied by a generator and he heard a television blasting inside the home. The noise and the light was a constant reminder that he was an outsider. He also knew their electricity, fun and television were happening because of his hard work in the fields. He was a restavek. An outcast. Someone who didn't belong. He was someone selfishly used to take care of the needs of others.

He watched hungrily as the children brought food outside to their dog and petted him. Evens hated that dog because the dog ate better than he did. His anger grew to the point of thinking, *I wonder what dog meat might taste like.*

The farmer had two pigs tied to the depot. Evens fed them the food scraps from the home and the pigs kept getting larger. He knew that soon one of them would be butchered and he wouldn't be able to eat any of the meat.

One evening, he was able to watch a voodoo ceremony from a distance. With the drums beating, the alcohol flowing and the dancing going on and on into the night, he saw a goat being sacrificed. He returned to the depot again seething with anger and hunger. He thought, *oh, how I'd love to have just a piece of that goat meat!*

Evens hunger, anger and hatred continued to grow. He desperately started dreaming of a way to control at least some aspect of his life.

Chapter 31

Joseph

Alix had thoroughly enjoyed alcohol and the wild nightlife. His partying led to other activities with women other than his wife.

Early in their marriage his wife had asked him about where he was always going and what he was doing. The beatings he gave her eventually took care of the questions and complaining.

The small odd jobs he received had provided the funds for his alcohol and other activities. That left very few gourdes for his wife and three children to live on. Fortunately his wife was good at gardening so they had corn, beans and eggplant growing at home. Random mangoes and bananas periodically helped fill empty stomachs.

His lifestyle didn't leave much time for his children. In his opinion, raising children was a 'woman's job.'

For the last year he'd been noticing a few things changing. He was having ongoing diarrhea, coughing spells and had developed sores in his mouth that hurt horribly. He noticed his pants didn't fit like they had before, so he began using a piece of rope in the loops to keep them from falling. When he mentioned his health issues to his wife, she'd said, "I've noticed some of the same things happening with me."

Life continued as they both continued getting weaker and losing more weight. The children were now six, five and four-years-old. The parents relied more and more on them to take care of the garden, getting water, washing the clothes, and preparing the food.

Alix finally became so weak he couldn't get out of bed. His oldest son, six-year-old Joseph, had to help him use the toilet and lately Joseph was having to feed him as well.

Joseph watched his mom losing weight and strength at the same time. She was rapidly failing.

~

When his papa died, there wasn't any money for a funeral or a spot in the cemetery crypt, so Joseph and his brother dug a hole behind their garden to bury their father. Joseph felt nothing as he shoved his father into the hole and covered him with dirt.

With impending doom, Joseph watched his mother deteriorate over the next month. He and his brother dug another grave. This time they gently edged their mama into the ground. They covered her with an old sheet before reluctantly and carefully adding the dirt. Both boys wept.

Joseph would learn much later that AIDS was a disease making inroads in his beautiful country of Haiti. He would know his parents had succumbed to the horror of the HIV virus and the subsequent disease of AIDS. Over two percent of the population, 200,000 people, were living with HIV/AIDS.

Most of the very poor and rural people lived in denial as to its presence in their lives. Though the Antiretroviral Therapy medicines were freely available to help control symptoms, admitting to HIV/AIDS was culturally unacceptable. Thus, deaths were occurring without intervention.

After burying their mother, the women and families in the lakou helped care for the two youngest children. Joseph was taken in by an aunt who lived miles away in another village.

The aunt knew about AIDS and was angry that her brother-in-law had infected and taken the life of her only sister.

When Joseph arrived at his aunt's home, she said, "Joseph, I promised my sister I'd take care of you. I keep my promises."

Joseph felt secure and safe.

For a while things went well for Joseph. His aunt provided food and a bed. She had said when school started in October, he could go. He helped with the chores around the house and in reality his life was better now than it had been at home. He missed his mama, little sister and brother, but rarely thought about his papa.

Then, tragedy struck as Joseph became ill. It began with a small fever, then a cough and wheezing. His aunt changed. She screamed at six-year-old Joseph, "What have you brought into my house?"

Joseph, with a puzzled look, said, "What do you mean?"

"Your mama and papa died of 'the disease' and now you bring it here to me and my family?"

"I don't know what you mean."

Angrily, with fear in her eyes, she grabbed him by the neck and took him to the back yard. Giving him a blanket and a plate, she led him to the cooking shelter.

"Stay in the yard!"

She went to the house and closed the back door.

Dazed, Joseph had no idea what had just happened other than the clue about 'the disease.'

He assumed his aunt was talking about the sickness that claimed the life of his mama and papa.

Twice the next day, food was left for him on the back step of the house. The following day he was feeling better. The fever was gone and he was coughing less and less. He stayed in the yard.

Two more days came and went.

When his aunt came the next time to the back yard, Joseph said, "I don't have a fever and I'm not coughing anymore. Can I move back into the house?"

With a glare, she said, "Absolutely not. I've seen this before. The fever will come and go just like your cough. You have what my sister and your papa had. It's a dangerous and contagious disease."

With that she disappeared into the house and Joseph was alone once again.

~

Evens frantically dug in the dirt with his hands. He was trying desperately to find what he'd lost. His hands hurt. His eyes stung from his tears. It began to rain. The dirt became wet and turned to mud, so he scooped faster and faster. Water filled his hole and the mud caved in as the rain continued to pour down.

Joseph woke up from the nightmare. His face was wet and it was really raining. He hated the dream which he was having over and over again.

He stood, gathered his wet blanket and moved to the side of the tree that was drier. Sitting on the wet blanket with his back leaning against the tree, he found himself still getting wet. He moved to the cooking area and huddled under the overhanging tin.

As he listened to the rain hitting the tin, he realized he wouldn't be able to sleep with the ongoing patter. So, he began rolling through the memories of his young life. He realized there weren't any good memories, just the memories which brought the dreaded nightmares. He couldn't believe how the days and weeks rolled by so slowly. He wondered how long he'd be held captive in the dreaded and hated yard.

The lack of adequate food and the absence of decent shelter weren't the only difficulties in his young life. He was bored as there was simply nothing to do, all day and all night, except for fitful sleep. But the most difficult thing began on a day when a neighbor stopped by the house and talked to him. The man reached down and patted Joseph on the top of his head and then left.

Almost immediately his aunt came into the yard with a broom. Holding it by the bristle end, she swung the handle at Joseph hitting him on his ear. Then, another swing caught him on his ribs. He screamed and cowered under the roof of the cooking shelter. His ear was dripping blood. Fear had unleashed something evil in his aunt's mind.

Then, she said, "You have 'the disease' and you're not to touch anyone or let anyone touch you. I'll not let you infect anyone else!" With that she went into the house.

Those entering the yard after that would always wonder why the small boy would shrink away from them like a beaten puppy. He became an untouchable. The absence of touch was absolutely the worst thing Joseph had to endure.

Dawn came and the rain stopped. As he looked around the yard, which was now his home, he saw trash and mud. With an angry glance, he looked at the house and knew things were dry and clean inside.

His aunt brought him breakfast an hour later. She had looked at him with disdain and disgust as she set the small plate of food and the glass of water on the step. She angrily said, "I made a promise to your mama to take care of you. But it never occurred to me the promise could mean disease and death for my family."

That afternoon, he felt chills even though the sun was sharing its heat unmercifully. He felt the fever coming back and by dusk, he was coughing again. When his aunt brought the evening meal, she said, "I heard you coughing. Are you sick again?"

Joseph said, "I'm not feeling well. Being in the rain last night made me sick."

"That isn't what made you sick. Look at me. I'm not sick. My neighbors aren't sick. Yet, you're sick... again! I know what the problem is and it's not the rain!"

He knew it was useless to say any more. He couldn't believe his own aunt would treat him like a common dog.

The next day, Joseph's aunt had a solution. She took Joseph on a ten minute walk to another hut. A man emerged from the small home and said, "Ah, so this is Joseph?"

His aunt replied, "Yes, he's the one I told your wife about. His mama and papa died and he's without a home."

Joseph coughed once, twice, three times. The man skeptically asked, "Are you sick?"

Before Joseph could answer, his aunt said, "No, he caught a fever because he spent too much time playing in the rain yesterday. He's fine. He's a great worker. He's still small, but he knows how to work. Sometimes he needs a bit of encouragement, but he'll work hard for you."

The man shook his aunt's hand and Joseph saw something subtly being passed into her hand as they gripped.

His aunt smiled broadly as she left the man's lakou and without a goodbye to Joseph she headed back to her home.

The man's name was Jean and his wife was Chedeline. They'd been unable to have children.

Materially however, they had been fortunate. They'd inherited three acres of land from his father who had inherited it from his father. On those three acres they successfully grew corn. They also had a mill that ground the corn into meal, which they were able to sell in the area markets.

Other people brought their corn to them for grinding, so all of those sources of income helped them live a life better than most.

Over the next several months, a few things became apparent to Joseph.

First, he had to work very hard for the couple. He'd never felt so exhausted in his young life, but secretly he enjoyed working alongside Jean. He almost cried the day Jean put a large, rough hand on Joseph's head and said, "Son, you're doing a great job for me."

Secondly, since they had wanted children throughout their marriage, Joseph seemed to be an answer to prayer for them. They seemed to enjoy having Joseph around.

Thirdly, his situation at their home was incredibly better than the hell he'd endured at his aunt's home. She was his own flesh and blood, yet there was a cruelty in her that he couldn't explain.

Though his aunt had told him continually that he was sick with 'the disease', he'd never felt better. He was beginning to think he was normal. His strength was growing as Chedeline encouraged him to eat until he was full.

His months as a yard-kid seemed distant. Jean and Chedeline let him sleep in the house and eat his meals with them. He was feeling blessed, but he was holding his breath, waiting for the next shoe to drop.

Chapter 32

Evens

Evens had a plan and he began collecting the resources to put it into action. This was truly going to be a degaje project, a real "making do" opportunity. If there was one thing he'd learned in his young and desperate life, it was how to survive by 'making do.'

His plan was driven partly by hunger while the other part was purely selfish and vindictive. His internalized anger prompted a rebellious desire to do something that would exert control and try to do it in total secrecy of his master.

One night while lying awake in the quietness of the depot, he remembered something someone had once told him. The story related to the process of catching a mongoose for food. He had never eaten mongoose but he knew many poor people did. He sometimes saw mongoose running through the brush behind the depot. They were extremely fast and elusive, but Evens thought he'd try his hand at trapping one.

He finally had all the necessary items he needed. Two pieces of string, a stake, and a small tree branch with a V on one end. He hid them in the depot. He also knew he'd need the machete which hung on the depot wall as well as the large basket made of bamboo and interwoven reeds. The most important thing he needed was stolen earlier that afternoon from his master. He had been able to separate a chick from its protective mother. Now he had his bait.

Finally, night came. He waited until the house was dark and the dog was quiet. He crept behind the depot where earlier he'd seen a mongoose. Quietly, he pushed the stake in the ground and tied a short string to it. He tied both legs of the peeping chick to the string attached to the stake. Then he tied another string around both legs again and tied it to the V stick.

Next, he propped the basket with the V stick to keep the basket from falling. One side of the basket was on the ground with the other suspended four inches above the ground. He knew the mongoose could slip under the basket, grab the peeping chick which would drop the basket and seal its fate.

He sat excitedly behind the depot watching and waiting. In his mind he wondered what the broiled mongoose would taste like. He also had time to think about his mama and four siblings. He tried to remember what life had been like when his papa was alive. The months since his papa's death had taken a toll on his memories. Sitting quietly in the night waiting for dinner, Evens wasn't pleased with some of the angry thoughts rolling around in his mind.

Then, he heard a noise. Something was moving in the dark. He heard the chick peeping. Then he heard a low rumbling growl and the basket being knocked out of the way. A stray dog had found the chick.

Angrily, he gathered his gear and took it to the depot. His greatest fear now was worrying the family would realize a chick was gone.

Undeterred, he tried again the following night. No dog. No mongoose. Another long night.

On the third night, he saw a fleeting glimpse of a mongoose in the brush. There was a quick peep and the basket fell. He quickly rushed to hold down the basket as the mongoose wanted out, and it wanted out 'now!'

Evens realized he'd made a mistake. The machete was still in the depot. He had no way to deal with an angry mongoose and he didn't want to get bit. So, carefully he lifted the basket an inch. That was all that was needed as the mongoose wedged its way out with the chick in its mouth. It blasted out of the basket, ran between his legs and was gone.

Angrily, he gathered his equipment and headed to the depot. This time however, he knew his plan had worked! He also knew there was a local mongoose with a taste for baby chicks.

Though he was losing a lot of sleep, he was determined to see this through to the finish. There was more at stake than satisfying his physical hunger. He needed to succeed at getting the best of his master.

~

Two nights later, sacrificing the third stolen chick, his machete caught the mongoose on its escape from the overturned basket. Though he had never butchered anything in his seven-year-old life, the machete served him well in skinning and butchering the oversized rodent.

Making a small fire with sticks he had gathered over the last week and a stolen match from the cooking area, the broiling began. A few hours before dawn, his physical hunger was satisfied and he felt incredibly empowered and confident. He had succeeded in surviving with his own skills.

Back in the depot with all the evidence of his adventure buried or hidden, he slept for the first time in six months with a confident, self-satisfied smile on his face.

The next morning he rose to a dawn that mirrored his mood. A beautiful sunrise welcoming a new day.

He decided to time his twice daily trip to the village pump to coincide with two of his restavek friends. He couldn't wait to share his story of bravery and rebellion!

Arriving at the pump he saw Rose in line with her buckets waiting for water. Soon, Jesulah arrived. He told them, "Don't hurry off. I have something to tell you before you leave."

After Jesulah pumped her water, she joined Rose and Evens on the path. Before he began sharing his story, two boys came down the trail. Evens hadn't met them before, but Jesulah and Rose, both with wide smiles, simultaneously said, "Hey Jean Pierre. How are you?"

"I'm doing fine. You know how life is. But I'm always concerned about both of you. I know life is a lot more difficult for the two of you than it is for me. Are you doing okay?"

Rose said, "I'm doing okay."

Jesulah replied, "It's still the same. I don't think things will ever be okay until I'm no longer a restavek."

Then she continued, "Jean Pierre, do you know Evens?"

Jean Pierre looked at Evens and said, "No, but I've seen him around."

Rose asked Jean Pierre, "Who do you have with you? Someone new coming to our village pump?"

"Oh, this is Joseph. He lives in the countryside on the other side of the village. He just turned seven-years-old. His mama and papa died so he became a restavek. He's had some really tough times, but things are improving."

Evens felt a twinge of envy as he heard things were going well for Joseph.

Then Jesulah said, "Oh, Jean Pierre, Evens was just going to tell us something."

Evens shared his mongoose story with Rose, Jesulah, Jean Pierre and Joseph, but he felt a bit awkward as the story seemed a bit anti-climactic and trivial. He had thought the two girls would be impressed with his story, and they were, but the two boys didn't seem very captivated.

Evens asked Jean Pierre, "How long have you been a restavek?"

"I lost my family in the earthquake, so it's been several years. I'm now thirteen-years-old."

He continued, "Evens, I know how good it feels to secretly have power over your master, but there's always a price to pay. It may feel good now, but the rigoise isn't far behind. Restaveks have no advocates. There's no one standing beside you or helping you when you're in trouble. When trouble comes, you'll stand alone. Be careful."

The five friends parted and went on their way to their respective homes and the waiting, never-ending work.

Evens had felt confident and pleased, yet Jean Pierre's words definitely caused some of that confidence to diminish. Jean Pierre seemed older, wiser and showed genuine concern. Evens thought it would probably be wise to listen to his advice. Yet, there was still a part of him anxious to again test his newfound independence.

~

Dusk and then darkness came to the field behind the depot. He had been looking forward to another mongoose roasting over open flames. He decided to put Jean Pierre's advice to the side.

The trap was set and the chick was peeping. In the light of the moon, he watched intently. Evens felt a twinge of guilt as he realized another chick was inadvertently calling in his executioner.

He waited. Suddenly he heard a noise behind him. He turned around in time to see a wooden stick being swung in the hands of his farmer-master.

Then, things went black.

He awoke on the floor of the depot. A candle eerily lit the darkness. Groggily looking around, he saw the angry farmer sitting on a chair with the stick in his hand.

Evens quickly scooted away, but the farmer stood up and towered over him. Swinging the stick again and again, Evens screamed in pain as he was hit on his ribs, legs, arms and head.

Tiring, the farmer sat in the chair and said, "Now I know what's been happening to my chicks."

Evens whimpered but said nothing.

"At first, I thought a mongoose was getting in at night and stealing them. Now I know what's happened. The mongoose was getting my chicks, but he had a helper."

Evens whimpered, watched and waited.

The farmer continued, "Evens, this is your first and only chance. If anything like this ever happens again, you'll be very, very sorry. Chicken thieves, when caught the first time are beaten. The second time, it isn't a rigoise or stick you'll see, but a machete. There are no second chances!"

He left.

Evens curled into a fetal position, thought about Jean Pierre's words earlier that day and cried.

The next day, nursing his bruises, Evens approached the group of children at the pump. All were looking at the two knots on his head. They had been chattering loudly as he arrived, but it turned into a dead silence as they stared at him.

Rose asked, "Evens, are you okay? We heard what happened." She went to him and put her arm around his shoulder and looked at his bruises and lumps.

Evens, ashamed, said, "I'll be okay, but I'm scared."

Another boy said, "You should be. People are talking about you in the village. You're being called a chicken thief. Everyone knows."

Someone else said, "You better hope chickens don't disappear around the village. We know who they'll blame!"

Evens waited in line, finally got his water and headed back to the farmers home. A knot of fear gripped his stomach. He stopped along the side of the path and vomited.

~

Though he was incredibly busy with his work for the farmer, Evens couldn't escape the dark cloud hanging over his head. Stealing the chicks had seemed like a smart thing to do at the time. Eating the mongoose had been a sweet victory of independence, or so it had seemed.

But, as the days slowly plodded along, he still remembered Jean Pierre's parting statement. *'Restaveks have no advocates. There's no one standing beside you or helping you when you're in trouble. When trouble comes, you'll stand alone. Be careful.'*

Another dawn pushed its way into Evens precious sleep. Groggily he woke and forced himself up from the depot floor.

Immediately he went to the fields to begin his work. The mornings were always cooler and he tried to get most of his field work completed before noon. Hoeing, watering, cutting, gathering and carrying. He was getting very good at the never ending manual labor.

He returned to the depot to gather two buckets and then headed to the village pump. He was pleased to see there were ten or so children already in line. That gave him the opportunity to talk to friends and to rest. Working in the field non-stop for six hours had taken a toll.

Finally with filled buckets, he headed down the path to the depot. It was a ten minute walk requiring him to stop and rest periodically along the way.

There was a wooded area where he typically rested in the shade. Setting his buckets of water on the ground, he laid down and rested. Looking up at the leaves of the bamboo, mango and banana trees, he felt peaceful.

Then he heard men talking, coming his direction. He stood up and saw two men coming down the path. He knew them from the village.

When the men saw Evens, they stopped and looked at one another. They came toward him and the taller man said, "Talk about the devil and there he is."

The other man laughed and said, "It's almost funny. We've been looking for you. We were hoping we'd find you."

"Why were you looking for me?"

The taller one said, "I lost two chickens last night. Everyone in the village knows who the chicken thief is."

"We know you stole chicks from the farmer. Everyone knew you wouldn't steal from him again because of the beating he gave you. But we also know, once someone is a thief, it's only a matter of time until they steal again. Chicken thieves develop a taste for chicken, just like a mongoose!"

The black cloud suddenly engulfed Evens once again.

The shorter man grabbed Evens arm and swung him to the ground.

Evens looked up at the two men with terror in his eyes. "I didn't steal your chickens. I promise. I only took chicks so I could catch a mongoose. I was almost starving and I was desperate. I didn't steal your chickens."

"Yeah, right. There's no way we'll believe that."

"I promise. I didn't steal your chickens. Someone else did it, knowing I'd get blamed. Everyone in the village knows I'll get the blame so they have nothing to lose by stealing your chickens." Then pleading with a quivering voice, he said quietly, "Give me a chance. I might be able to find out who did it."

The tall man slapped Evens on the face. Then both men started hitting him. He screamed. Suddenly, a balled up fist hit him on his head.

Evens almost passed out, but the beating continued. Limply, he continued to receive the blows and kicks from the men. He whimpered and cried.

Then it was over. The beating stopped. Evens touched his forehead and looked at his blood covered fingers. He knew he was bleeding from multiple wounds.

He looked up at the men thinking it was over. Then he screamed when he saw the short man pull a knife from his pocket. He flipped the long blade open. Evens again screamed in horror, "Please don't, please don't...!"

Suddenly, someone shouted, "Stop! What are you doing?"

Turning his head, he got a glimpse of Rose coming down the path with a bucket in her hand. She was screaming, "Stop. Stop! Don't hurt him!"

The tall man grabbed her by her arm and said, "Girl, this is none of your business. Leave!"

"Evens is my friend and you have no right to hurt him!"

"He's a chicken thief and he was warned there'd be trouble for him if he stole again. He's taken two of my chickens. Now he has to pay. He's a chicken thief."

Rose bravely stood between Evens and the men and said, "You can't do that. He's just a boy. If restavek families would feed their restaveks, boys like him wouldn't have to steal to satisfy their hunger."

Then she said loudly, "Run, Evens, run!"

Evens quickly stood and ran down the path, leaving his water buckets behind. He glanced back in time to see the men beating Rose who was now lying on the ground.

Evens got to the depot and caught his breath. His forehead was still bleeding but it wasn't serious. His ribs and legs hurt horribly from the kicks, but he knew it would have been worse if Rose had not shown up.

He hoped she had gotten away before being badly hurt. Yet, now he was feeling enormous guilt. He knew she was innocent, yet she had purposely taken his place.

Evens knew he needed to do something for Rose. Yet, he knew if he returned to the area, the two men would stab him and likely beat him to death. Frantically, he ran to Joanna's hut.

He knew she cared about Rose, so he thought possibly she could help.

Pounding on her door, he impatiently yelled, "Joanna! Joanna!"

The door opened and Joanna saw a small boy in tears and asked, "What's wrong?"

"Rose was beaten by two men and I'm afraid for her." Pointing up the path, he desperately said, "Can you find her and make sure she's okay? Please?"

He continued, "I can't go. The two men were beating me and then pulled a knife. I think they were going to cut off my hand or maybe even kill me. They think I stole their chickens. Rose stopped them and now they're hurting her."

Without a thought she hurried up the path. Evens stood at the door and watched, surprised at how fast the old woman could move. Slowly he walked toward the depot.

Chapter 33

Rose

Ah, the memories were sweet. As sweet as the sugarcane her papa had given her when she left home. As sweet as the river-bank time she had spent with her mama when she was five. As sweet as the times her papa had told her of the proverbs of long-gone African slaves. As sweet as the times her papa told her she'd be wise, just and compassionate. As sweet as the time her mama told her she'd someday care for the last, lost, least and lonely.

Rose's eyes opened. Weakly she looked around the small hut which was filled with the light of another day. Her eyes met the eyes of the old woman.

Joanna was holding Rose's hand and pressing a wet, cool cloth to her forehead.

She weakly asked, "How long have I been sleeping?"

"It's been a night, a day and another night."

Joanna said, "Rose, you've been hurt very badly. Two men beat you horribly and then one of them stabbed you. I'm doing the best I can to take care of you."

She continued, "I've told Jude you won't be coming back to him and that I'll care for you. He said it's okay because he can't take care of an injured girl." Then she smiled and said, "So, it looks like you can live with me after all."

There was no more talking. Then there was a quiet rapping at the hut's door. Joanna slowly rose from her usual kneeling position by Rose and went to the glassless window. She pulled back the small cloth covering the opening and peered outside. She was concerned that those who had stabbed and beaten Rose would return to finish their work.

Instead, four children stood in her yard. The concern on their familiar faces was an indication of their love for Rose. She opened the door.

The girl said, "We heard Rose is staying with you. She's our friend. Is she here?"

Joanna looked at Evens and said, "Evens, it looks like your cuts and bruises are healing."

Then looking at the others, she asked, "Who are the rest of you?"

"I'm Jesulah."

"My name is Jean Pierre."

"...and I'm Joseph."

"How do you children know her?

Jean Pierre started by saying, "I've known her for a long time. Usually we talked in the market but I would often see her at the well. She's been a good friend."

"We first met three years ago at the water pump. We were both getting water. We've been as close as sisters," said Jesulah.

Joseph said, "When I first came to this village, many people treated me very badly. But Rose was one who always treated me with kindness."

Evens stood to the side.

Joanna said, "What about you Evens? How did you first come to know Rose?"

Even's eyes filled with tears. He couldn't speak.

Pausing, Joanna said, "Rose is very, very sick. I've been caring for her for two days. The beating she took from the two men and the knife stabbing they gave her were very bad. She's getting weaker and weaker. She needs her rest. I'll ask if she wants to see you."

She closed the door and knelt beside Rose. Before she could say anything, Rose tried to sit up and whispered, "I heard my friends. Can I see them?"

The old woman opened the door and cautiously the four children approached Rose. Rose's dry and cracked lips parted in an awkward smile.

The old woman said, "That's the first smile I've seen on Rose's face in two days. You children are good medicine."

Weakly, Rose tried to pull herself up again on her elbow but fell with pain to her burlap mattress. She said, "I'm so happy to see you. You've all been my best friends."

Jesulah began to cry as she saw the pain on Rose's face. She asked Joanna if she could hold the cloth on Rose's forehead.

Handing the cloth to Jesulah, she dipped it in the basin of water, wrung it out and patted Rose's face. Jesulah's tears flowed down her face.

Then Evens quietly said to Joanna, "Madame Joanna, you asked me how I came to know Rose?"

He knelt down by the bed. His face was inches away from Rose. She saw the tears spilling down his cheeks.

With a quivering voice he said, "Rose, you saved my life. If you hadn't come along when you did, the two men would have kept beating me and probably killed me. I was a chicken thief, but didn't steal from them. You didn't need to do it, but you took my place. You didn't do anything to those men. You were innocent and I was guilty. I should be the one lying on this bed with the stab wounds. It should be me. I don't know what to say. I don't deserve having a friend like you. Thanks Rose for taking my place and showing me love."

Rose said, "Evens, you've always been like family to me. All of you have. I didn't have to think more than a second about what I did for you Evens. It just came naturally because I loved you and didn't want to see you being hurt. I'd do it all over again."

Jesulah said, "Rose, I'm so sorry for what you've gone through. I wanted to come and thank you for being my friend. You know what I've gone through and yet you've still loved me and always cared about me. You've always asked me how I'm doing. It meant a lot to know there was someone who cared. When times were the worst, I knew you understood because you've been through those tough times too."

She continued, "Oh, you should know I've followed your advice. Any chance I've had on Sunday's, I sat outside the window of the church and listened to what was being said." Then she paused, not knowing if she should or could continue, "It was like the pastor was talking about you."

Rose said, "What do you mean?"

Jesulah said, "The pastor was always talking about Jesus, but it sounded like he was talking about you. The pastor said Jesus had to leave his Father's house. He didn't want to leave the love in his home, because his Father loved Him so much and he loved his Father the same way. But, his Father asked his son Jesus to leave Heaven to help the last, least, lost and lonely. Jesus knew He had to leave his home to help those who couldn't help themselves. There was no other way for his Father to help those who were lost. He had to send someone who knew the way. Jesus knew.

He left his home because he was obedient and because he loved his Papa. I think He must have been like a restavek. He came to live with another family. As he got older, he had three years of helping others, just like you. Three years of serving.

Jesus seemed to be constantly walking. He didn't have a pillow to lay his head on. He didn't know where his next food would come from. He never knew which friend would betray him for their own good. I think Jesus was like a restavek.

He was a leader. He was full of compassion. He stood against those who were doing wrong. He cried with others, healed others, and did whatever his Papa asked him to do. It was never easy for him. He was abused, tortured and injured because he never stopped doing what was right. It was like the pastor was talking about you, Rose, when he spoke about Jesus. All of that makes me think that Jesus was like a restavek."

Then, Jesulah began crying. Joanna put her arms around her and held her. Finally, Jesulah stopped crying. Rose said, "Jesulah, are you okay?"

Jesulah waited a full minute before answering. "I don't know if I can keep talking about what I heard."

Rose said, "Please, please. I want to hear!"

Jesulah continued, "There came a time when evil men with selfish ideas hurt Jesus very badly. They eventually..."

Rose said, "Yes, I know the story."

"But Rose, it's hard for me to say they killed Him. Because He was so innocent and yet He was willing to take their place and die for them."

"Yes, I know. It's difficult because you're worried about me dying?"

"Yes, you seem really weak. I can't bear the thought of losing you."

Rose said with a smile, "But, you remember the rest of the story about Jesus, right? Even though he bled and died, he rose and went to be with His Papa again. As weak as I am and the way I feel, I don't think I'm going to live long. But when I go, I know I'll be in a place where I'll see Jesus and his Papa." Then with a weak smile, "I think someday I'll see all of you again."

Epilogue

Jesulah, Jean Pierre, Evens and Joseph stood together in the small cemetery. The green and white above-ground, plastered tombs were scattered irregularly in a small pasture. A cow was tied to the cross of one tomb. Two small, naked boys were sitting on another. Someone's wash was drying on a third.

The old woman Joanna had selflessly given her own cemetery crypt for the burial of Rose. She had said, "I know I'll need it soon, but Rose deserves it more than I do, or anyone else I know."

The sad and ragged four, shared memories as they spoke of their friend, Rose the restavek. Each had a smile as they said the words, 'Rose the restavek.' Always before, the word restavek meant something bad, now they each had a new perspective about restavek. The life of Rose the restavek had taught them about Jesus.

Jesus had been the poorest of the poor. He didn't even have a pillow to lay his head on! He was the one who was last, least, lost and lonely. Now the four restavek children had an advocate. Someone who had been through the tough times. Someone who always came out of His battles victorious, with scars, with hurt, but with a peace no one could take away. One who conquered a world full of evil and left redemption, peace and love in its place.

Jesulah said, "I'm thinking Jesus's Papa has a better plan for children than becoming a restavek. I think there's coming a day when orphans or vulnerable children will be treated like family. I don't think Rose died without purpose. Maybe people who have restavek children will begin treating them like their own children. Maybe people like James and Marie Lucie will be punished in this country for what they do.

She continued, "There might be a time when neighbors will stand up for the restavek children being abused in their lakou. I remember what the pastor said one Sunday in his sermon as I listened under the window. He said, "The Bible says in St. Luke 17:2, *'It would be better if a large stone was tied around a man's neck and he'd be thrown into the sea, than for him to cause one of these little ones to be hurt.'*"

Jesulah paused and said, "Maybe the life of Rose the restavek will help others know about Jesus. Maybe her death will change the future for all restaveks. I know that's what God wants.

"I'll never forget her last words to us, 'I think someday I'll see all of you again.'"

~

The sun was setting as the four restavek children walked together down the path. Soon, each would peel off from the group to go to their respective homes and the waiting work. Most likely some of them would be punished with a rigoise and no evening meal for being late. But, as Jesulah said to the others, "It'll be worth it!"